THOSE BURIED TEXANS

Hendrick-Long Publishing Company
P.O. Box 12311
Dallas, Texas 75225

Library of Congress Catalog Card Number 80-82288
ISBN 0-937-46000-1

INTRODUCTION

Approximately 25,000 years ago, man first recognized himself as unique among living creatures. At the same time, he became aware that he did not exist alone or in isolation from those like him. Contact with other humans convinced him that existence was easier and safer when he moved and lived in groups rather than in solitude. The subsequent interaction with his own kind caused man eventually to take some care with those who had ceased life. Increased concern for living man brought about increased awareness of honoring man's remains. Man began to bury his dead, protecting them rather than leaving them exposed to wild animals and the elements.

At this point in man's social evolution, theologians believe that man began to worship phenomena in nature, which at first he greatly feared or could not understand. In this context, man developed awareness of his own soul, a spiritual kinship with the world around him. From this awareness of self, man progressed to the idea of a supreme creator, responsible not only for man's world, but also for man himself.

Once man decided that he was the unique creation of a supreme creator, his concern for care after death increased. Manifestations of future elaborate concern for the dead emerge simply enough in early man's depositing the remains of the dead in a safe place: under the ground, in a cave, or on a stilted platform. The safety of the remains equated with man's sense of honor regarding the deceased as a fellow human; as a part of man's own relationship with the supreme creator. From simple procedures, care of the dead soon grew into extravagant efforts lasting great periods of time and involving elaborate tombs.

The locations of the places of burial were highly sacred. In American Indian cultures, a designated place of burial might be used over and over by different transient groups with the deceased being placed on a level above each previous group and would, in time, create a "mound-like" configuration. This burial phenomenon shows man's curious combination of fear and respect for the unbreakable chain of existence from earth, to life, to earth again.

Events, natural or otherwise, might often denote cause for the sacredness of a particular location or for the selection of proper sites for those now dead form a "sturdy race that had passed before." In days past, intended cremation was restricted to two basic considerations: to denote total defeat of an enemy or to dispose of unacceptable members of a society, such as an infant with a birth defect. In the latter case, the child would ceremonially be put to death, cremated and buried, generally in a special locality of the tribe concerned.

Indian burials many times show belief in an afterlife through the position of the body interred: face up or buried in a fetal state with the face toward the east awaiting the first day of the hereafter. In some cases, the dead were placed in a standing position.

Special honor has always been afforded those in leadership roles, both in ancient Egypt and in more recent society, for here the suspicion has existed, until recent times, that there is a strong connection between leadership and the divine (i.e., the Divine Right or Appointment of Kingship). Placement at the "head" of a communal burial configuration pattern or, as today, within cathedral vaults or places of national designation is common for those who have held celebrated positions in society.

In modern times man has not greatly changed his thoughts with regard to burials despite space-age knowledge and nuclear capabilities. He buries for about the same reasons as did his ancestors: love of memory, religious meanings, honor, fear, cultural dictates and sanitation. Like those before him, modern man selects designated locations, considering availability, proximity to loved ones, will requests, scenic aspects, drainable and stabe land conditions. Services attending the "last rites" vary in length and composition from nothing save placement of the remains in a designated area to long and elaborate services with much motion and ado. Most societies place the remains in some container; however, some societies do not. The Indian does not contain the body on every occasion. Those who leave the bodies uncontained within the earth say that they are giving the body back to mother earth and that this is the opportunity for them to repay the earth for what they, in life, have taken from the soil.

Tombstones themselves have had an evolution all their own: from the simple rock at the head and foot, fashioned only by nature, to the most ornate and artistic of gems to the flat, perpetual care, bronze slabs symbolizing modern quality manufacturing and, of course, the need to mow grass without impediment. Cemeteries, burial sites, and tombstones are evidences of memory and testimonials to the fact that this man-manner of symbolizing memory will show man's coalescence with his fellow man and his continuing faith in resurrection.

The number of burials in Texas is, of course, in the unestimable millions considering Indian, forgotten pioneer, single and composite unmarked sites, family plots in places of forgotten isolation as well as perpetual sites of today. We know that when early communities and towns were planned, first location priority items were given to sites for churches, burial grounds, and schools. High on man's agenda of caring has long been how he deals with death in this life.

This volume is dedicated with humble respect to those who, although buried, have no known location today, save to God Almighty.

Behold, I shew you a mystery; We shall not all sleep, but we shall all be changed,
In a moment, in the twinkling of an eye, at the last trump: for the trumpet shall sound, and the dead shall be raised incorruptible, and we shall all be changed.

Corinthians 15:51-52
King James Version of the Bible

PREFACE

Heritage, I believe, is in the final sense the remembering of our past and of those who contributed to it; those who laid the foundation and framework from generation to generation. Some were impressive, astonishing contributors to society from whose collected acts we developed a culture. Some were not so visible — they built homes, raised families, and routinely tried to survive day to day. They were the quiet ones. Their names never reached a printed page and are remembered by only a few. But they too provided the culture with a cohesiveness not only necessary but also essential for the ongoing of the culture.

We all, however, pass in time, and our footprints of contribution erode from distinctly defined marks freshly made on a sandy beach to a smooth surface washed afresh but for someone's memory. What then remains, except memory? Generally, we all receive a marker as to where our last remains are laid. Yet, comparatively few records of these locations are chronicled into what John Nesbitt would call "Time's Passing Parade."

I was appalled at the lack of records of known internments or entombments for so many of those who held the torch and briefly dazzled us with their one-act play called life. Surely heritage is in part the physical honoring of those contributors and their contribution, and it would seem that a portion of that honor is at least knowing where the last drama was played in their behalf and where "taps" was blown for them.

Many of the sites included in this work were heretofore unknown locations. Hopefully, publishing their location and recalling the histories regarding them will stimulate a new interest in the enormity of the contributions which they gave and in the challenge which we have to give likewise. I suppose the challenge is for each of us to make his own contribution, to make his own footprints on the silicon beach of life-time.

So many have helped in the identification of site and correction of confused records that I cannot list all of them. Some most graciously gave me time on the telephone. Some did research. Certainly the most dear to me in life as well in effort on this volume is my wife, Jane; I can still see her moving through cemetery after cemetery in constant pursuit of answers and locations despite the pauses necessary for the removal of the not endangered species called the grass burr from her clothing. In addition, were the untold hours of typing. My daughter, Janice, and her friend, Fred Bell, took some of the pictures for the book. My son, Austin, also contributed. Without them, I would never have completed this work.

For the efforts of the many record clerks at so many cemeteries, my eternal thanks. Also, "thank you" to the people who most graciously helped me at the Archives at the University of Texas in Austin, the Texas Highway Department, the Austin-Travis County Public Library, the Southwestern Historical Wax Museum, the Dallas Public Library, the **Dallas Morning News**, and the **Dallas Times Herald**, the directors of so many museums and historical sites — all of these played a most significant role. A special feeling of appreciation is for the families of those passed; families who in many cases held the key to correct locations and were willing to share. Finally, to my publisher, Jim Long, who dared to embark upon such a project, thank you.

The criteria used in this work were changed several times during completion as conditions made necessary. Nonetheless, they are as follows:

1. Those included must have been men or women of significance in Texas History.
2. Those included must have burial sites that are reasonably accessible.
3. Due to the abundance of heroes of the "States War" and World Wars I and II, only those of very special note are cited. Only the veterans of the Battle of San Jacinto who actually participated in the battle are included.
4. Texas has a colorful history spanning several hundred years, and the number of contributors to its overall picture is immense. Not everyone could be included, so I used my judgement as a "connoisseur" of Texas History in the selection of those chosen.

THOSE BURIED TEXANS

BURIAL SITES OF NOTEWORTHY TEXANS
An Alphabetical Listing Of Known Locations

Abamillo, Juan
-1836

Perished defending the Alamo, March 6, 1836.

Abercrombie, Wiley A.
-1836

Massacred as one of Fannin's men at Goliad
Buried: Goliad.

Adair, A. Garland
1889-1966

Newspaper Editor, World War I Veteran, American Legion Commander, Instrumental in the creation of the Texas Memorial Museum in Austin; he was curator of History there until his retirement in 1959.
Buried: State Cemetery in Austin.

Adams, James Moss
-1836

Massacred as one of Fannin's men at Goliad
Buried: Goliad.

Adams, Nathan
1869-1966

Banker, First National Bank, Dallas; A major contributor to Scottish Rite Hospital for Crippled Children
Buried: Oak Grove Cemetery in Dallas.

Adams, Wayman
1883-1959

Internationally recognized portrait artist and teacher
Buried: Oakwood Cemetery, Austin.

Addison, Nathaniel
1811-1900

Soldier in Texas Army, 1836
Buried: Salem Cemetery, Irene, Hill County.

Aldrich, Collin
1801-1842

Veteran of San Jacinto
Buried: Aldrich Cemetery, 9 miles southwest of Crockett.

Aldridge, Isaac
-1836

Massacred as one of Fannin's men at Goliad
Buried: Goliad.

Aldridge, John
-1836

Massacred as one of Fannin's men at Goliad
Buried: Goliad.

Aldrich, Roy Wilkinson
1869-1955

Texas Ranger with the longest service record (1915-1947)
Buried: Oakwood Cemetery, Austin.

Alexander, Jerome B.
-1842

Veteran of the Siege of Bexar and the Battle of San Jacinto; 1st Regiment, Texas Volunteers, Company D; Killed in the Dawson Massacre
Buried: Monument Hill, LaGrange.

Allen, James L.
1815-1901

Defender of the Alamo until March 5, 1836, when Travis sent him to Goliad to ask James Fannin for aid; Scout for Deaf Smith, Indian fighter, Mayor of Indianola, Tax assessor for Calhoun County
Buried: Yoakum, Texas.

Allen, John Kirby
1819-1838

Co-founder of the city of Houston with his brother, Augustus Chapman Allen; At his own expense outfitted the ship **Brutus** for service in the Revolution; Congressman during the Republic; On President Burnet's staff with rank of major; Promoter of the H & TC Railroad
Buried: Founders' Cemetery Houston.

Allen, John M.
-1847

Regular infantry staff at San Jacinto under Henry Millard; Was with Lord Byron when the poet died at Missolongi on April 12, 1823; Galveston's first mayor; U. S. Marshal from time Texas joined the Union until his death
Buried: Episcopal Cemetery, Galveston.

Allen, Layton
-1836

Massacred as one of Fannin's men at Goliad
Buried: Goliad

Allen, Peter
-1836

Massacred as one of Fannin's men at Goliad
Buried: Goliad.

Allen, R.
-1836

Perished defending the Alamo, March 6, 1836.

Allen, Richard
-1911

Legislator, First Grand Master of Black Masons in Texas, Bridge builder, City alderman, Customs collector
Buried: Houston.

Allen, Samuel T.
-1838

Imprisoned with Travis at Anahuac, Representative in the First Congress, Killed by Indians
Buried: Belton.

Alley, James
-1842

Killed at Dawson Massacre
Buried: Monument Hill, LaGrange.

Alley, William, Jr.
1800-1869

Member of Austin's Old 300
Buried: Alleyton.

Alley, William, Sr.
1770-1826 (?)

Member of Austin's Old 300
Buried: Alleyton.

Allison, Alfred
-1836

Massacred as one of Fannin's men at Goliad
Buried: Goliad.

Allison, Wilmer Lee
1905-1977

Member of Texas Sports Hall of Fame for tennis; Internationally recognized, Coach at U. T. (1957-1972)
Buried: Oakwood Cemetery, Austin.

Allston, William L.
-1836

Massacred as one of Fannin's men at Goliad
Buried: Goliad.

Allred, James V.
1899-1959

Governor of Texas (1935-1939); Fought monopolies in business, Was for regulation of public utilities and progressive legislation in line with FDR, Reorganized parole board, Increased the scope of workman's compensation, Was appointed to federal judgeship by President Truman
Buried: Riverside Cemetery, Wichita Falls

Alsbury, Mrs. Horace (Juana Navarro)
-after 1857

Raised by Bowie's mother-in-law; With her sister, Gertrudis Navarro, was in the Alamo when it fell to Santa Anna's troops. One of the Mexican soldiers (who had known their father) recognized the sisters and they were spared. Mrs. Almaron Dickinson said the sisters left the Alamo under a flag of truce on the night of March 4, 1836. Sister of Jose Antonio Navarro, Married to Alejo Perez before marrying Dr. Horace Alsbury
Buried: Alsbury Cemetery, East of San Antonio

Alsbury, Young Perry
1814-1878

2nd Regiment, Texas Volunteers, Cavalry
Buried: Alsbury Cemetery, East of San Antonio.

Ames, Allison
-1836

Massacred as one of Fannin's men at Goliad
Buried: Goliad.

Anderson, Bill
1837-1927

Member of Quantrill's Raiders, Captured in Centralia, Missouri
Buried: Salt Creek, Brown County.

Anderson, Patrick H.
-1836

Massacred as one of Fannin's men at Goliad
Buried: Goliad.

Anderson, Samuel
-1836

Killed at Battle of Refugio during Texas Revolution
Buried: Mt. Calvary Cemetery in Refugio.

Anderson, Washington
1817-1894

Veteran of San Jacinto; 1st Regiment, Texas Volunteers, Co. C.; Farmer; Aided in organizing Williamson County; Founder, with others of Georgetown, Texas
Buried: Greenwood Cemetery in Austin.

Andrews, Jessie
1867-1919

1st Female student of University of Texas in Austin, 1st Female instructor at UT (30 years service), a Poet Laureate of Texas Women's Press Association
Buried: Austin.

Andrews, Richard
-1836

Veteran of Gonzales, Killed at the Battle of Concepcion
Buried: Richmond.

**Andross,
Miles De Forest**
-1836

Perished defending the Alamo, March 6, 1836 at age 27.

Archer, Branch Tanner
1790-1856

Revolutionary leader and legislator, Veteran of Battle of Gonzales, Delegate to Convention of 1833, Commissioner with William Wharton and Stephen Austin to the United States, Member of 1st Congress
Buried: Eagle Island Plantation, Brazoria County.

Armstrong, A. Joseph
1873-1954

Nationally known authority on Robert Browning
Buried: Waco.

Armstrong, John Barclay
1850-1913

Texas Ranger, Assisted in capture of King Fisher, Captured John Wesley Hardin, Helped rid the Southwest of desperadoes
Buried: Armstrong, Willacy County.

Armstrong, Mollie Wright
1875-1964

1st woman optometrist in Texas and 2nd in the U.S.; Wrote a history of optometry
Buried: Brownwood, Texas.

Armstrong, William S.
-1836

Killed at the Battle of Refugio in the Texas Revolution
Buried: Mt. Calvary Cemetery, Refugio.

Arnold, Hayden S.
1808-1839

Veteran of the Battle of San jacinto; 2nd Regiment, Texas Volunteers, Infantry; Member of the 1st Congress of the Republic; Indian negotiator
Buried: Oak Grove Cemetery, Nacogdoches.

Arnold, Hendrick
-1849

Free Negro; Came to Texas in 1826; Veteran of the Siege of Bexar with Ben Milam and of the Battle of San Jacinto; 2nd Regiment, Texas Volunteers, Cavalry; Member of Deaf Smith's spy company; Only other Black person at San Jacinto was Dick, a drummer
Buried: San Antonio.

Arnold, Ripley Allen
1817-1853

West Point graduate, Veteran of the Mexican War, 1st Commandant of Camp Worth.
Buried: Pioneer Rest Cemetery, Fort Worth.

Arrington, George W.
1844-1923

Served with John S. Mosby; Joined Maximillian forces in Mexico; Texas Ranger, Rancher, Sheriff of Wheeler, 1st and greatest peace officer of the Texas Panhandle
Buried: on his ranch, Mobeetie.

Austin, John
1801-1833

Member of Austin's Old 300
Buried: Brazoria.

Austin, Stephen Fuller
1793-1836

Greatest of the Empresarios; the Father of Texas; Well-educated for his time; Austin's genius, patience and perseverance brought about Texas' settlement and growth as an Anglo-American colony, republic and state; '...surely, there is not among men a more honorable destiny than to be the peaceful founder and builder of a new empire. . ."
Buried: State Cemetery, Austin.

Avery, Willis
1809-1888

Veteran of the Battle of San Jacinto; 1st Regiment, Texas Volunteers, Company C
Buried: Family Cemetery, 1 mile below Rices' Cemetery, Williamson County.

Autry, Micajah
-1836

Perished defending the Alamo, March 6, 1836.

Aynesworth,
Kenneth Hazen
1873-1944

Superintendent of John Sealy Hospital in Galveston, A founder of the Texas Surgical Society, Authority on Texas Archeology, Member of the Board of Regents of the University of Texas
Buried: Oakwood Cemetery, Waco.

Bacon, Sumner
1790-1844

Cumberland Presbyterian minister; Worked throughout East Texas; Distributed thousands of Bibles printed in English or Spanish; Unsalaried agent for the American Bible Society, Purchaser of ammunition in Houston's Army, 1st moderator of the Cumberland Synod of Texas
Buried: Chapel Hill Cemetery, San Augustine.

Badillo, Juan Antonio
-1836

Perished defending the Alamo, March 6, 1836.

Bagby, Arthur Pendleton
1833-1921

General in the Confederate Army, 5th Texas Cavalry; Practiced law in Victoria
Buried: Hallettsville.

Bagby, James S.
-1836

Massacred as one of Fannin's men at Goliad
Buried: Goliad.

Bailey, James Briton
1779-1833

Member of Austin's Old 300, Veteran of Battle of Velasco, Rank of Captain
Buried: Standing up with his gun, bullet mold, powder horn, hunting lantern and hound dog. Bailey's Prairie family cemetery, Munson Ranch between Angleton and West Columbia.

Bailey, Joseph Weldon
1863-1929

Lawyer, U.S. Congressman, Minority Leader of the House, Texas Senator; Accused but exonerated in the Waters-Pierce Oil Company case
Buried: Gainesville.

Bailey, Mollie Arline
1841-1918

Confederate spy and nurse; Operated a showboat on Mississippi River; With husband, Gus, created Bailey's Circus; Quit show business to take care of her

dying daughter
Buried: Houston.

Bailey, Peter James
-1836

Perished defending the Alamo, March 6, 1836, at age of 24.

Baine, Noel Moses
1800-1864

Veteran of the Battle of San Jacinto; 1st Regiment, Texas Volunteers, Company C
Buried: Prairie Lea Cemetery, Brenham.

Baines, George Washington
1809-1882

Early Baptist minister in Texas, President of Baylor University (1861-1863), Great-grandfather of Lyndon Baines Johnson
Buried: Salado.

Baird, Ninnie Lilla
1869-1961

Founder of Mrs. Baird's Bread Co.
Buried: Greenwood Cemetery, Ft. Worth.

Baird, Raleigh (M.D.)
1870-1941

A founder of the Dallas Medical and Surgical Clinic; Professor at Baylor College of Medicine; The Highland Park Methodist Church was organized in his home
Buried: Hillcrest Mausoleum, Dallas.

Baker, Augustus
-1836

Massacred as one of Fannin's men at Goliad
Buried: Goliad.

Baker, D. David D.
1806-1843

Veteran of the Siege of Bexar and of the Battle of San Jacinto; 1st Regiment, Texas Volunteers, Company D; Member of 1st Texas Congress
Buried: Matagorda County.

Baker, Daniel
1791-1857

Frontier Presbyterian minister, Educator, and 2nd President of Austin College
Buried: Huntsville (1st location of Austin College.)

Baker, Issac
-1836

Perished defending the Alamo; One of 32 from Gonzales who went to the defense of the Alamo, at age of 32.

Baker, Joseph
(Don Jose)
1804-1846

Veteran of the Battle of San Jacinto; 1st Regiment, Texas Volunteers, Company D; School teacher; With Gail Borden and Thomas Borden he founded **Telegraph and Texas Register** newspaper; Judge in Austin; Member of 1st and 2nd Congresses, Published **The Houstonian**
Buried: Oakwood Cemetery, Austin.

Baker, Moseley
1802-1848

Veteran of the Grass Fight and of Battle of Gonzales and Battle of San Jacinto; 1st Regiment, Texas Volunteers, Company D; Defender of San Felipe; Planter and lawyer; Member of the 1st, 3rd and 6th Congresses of the Republic; Methodist minister who founded the **True Evangelist** newspaper
Buried: State Cemetery, Austin.

Baker, Stephen
-1836

Massacred as one of Fannin's men at Goliad
Buried: Goliad.

Baker, William Charles
-1836

Perished defending the Alamo, March 6, 1836, Rank of captain.

Balch, John
1812-1900

Veteran of the Siege of Bexar and Battle of San Jacinto; 2nd Regiment, Texas Volunteers, Infantry
Buried: Chireno, Nacogdoches County or Cove Springs Cemetery, Nacogdoches County.

Ball, W. B.
1839-1923

Well-known Negro educator
Buried: Seguin.

Ballentine, John J.
-1836

Perished defending the Alamo, March 6, 1836.

Ballentine, Robert W.
-1836

Perished defending the Alamo, March 6, 1836, at age of 22.

Bancroft, Jethro Russell
-1848

Veteran of the Battle of San Jacinto; 2nd Regiment, Texas Volunteers, 5th Company (Thomas McIntire's Company)

Buried: Founders' Memorial Park, Houston.

Banks, Willette Rutherford
1881-1969

Negro Educator, Particularly instrumental in advancing Prairie View A&M University
Buried: Memorial Park, Prairie View.

Barbo, Antonio Gil Y
1729-1809

Founder of the city of Nacodoches
Buried: Old Spanish Cemetery, Nacogdoches.

Barclay, Robert
-1842
Barclay, Zed
-1842

Both killed at the Dawson Massacre
Buried: Monument Hill, LaGrange.

Barcley, John H.
-1836

Massacred as one of Fannin's men at Goliad
Buried: Goliad.

Barker, Eugene Campbell
1874-1956

Eminent historian at the University of Texas (1901-1951), Full professor there for 38 years; Among his works are: **Life of Stephen F. Austin, The Austin Papers, Readings in Texas History,** a series of public school textbooks; Managing editor of **The Southwest Historical Quarterly;** Instrumental in the origin of the University of Texas' Latin American and Littlefield Collections; Director of the Texas Historical Association
Buried: Oakwood Cemetery, Austin.

Barksdale, Eugene Campbell
1905-1974

Teacher and Professor of History, Author; Taught at the University of Texas at Arlington (1942-1971); Chairman of History Department there (1955-1971)
Buried: body donated to Southwestern Medical School at Dr. Barksdale's request.

Barnett, George Washington (M.D.)
1793-1838

Signer of the Texas Declaration of Independence, from South Carolina; Veteran of the Siege of Bexar; Senator

for six sessions during the Republic;
Killed by the Apaches
Buried: Old City Cemetery, Gonzales.

Barnett, Thomas
1798-1843

Signer of the Texas Declaration of
Independence, from Kentucky; Member
of Austin's Old 300
Buried: Family cemetery 5 miles N of
Rosenberg.

Barnhill, John N.
-1836

Massacred as one of Fannin's men
at Goliad
Buried: Goliad.

Barr, Alfred (Red)
1908-1971

Texas Sports Hall of Fame for Swimming; One of America's most successful
coaches; Guided SMU's swimming team
to 15 consecutive championships
Buried: Hillcrest Cemetery, Dallas.

Barr, Robert
1802-1839

Veteran of the Battle of San Jacinto;
2nd Regiment, Texas Volunteers, 4th
Company
Buried: Founders' Memorial Cemetery,
Houston.

Barret, Lyne Taliaferro
1832-1913

Bored the first producing oil well in
Texas in 1866 in Nacogdoches County at
Oil Springs — well 106 feet deep
Buried: Melrose, Texas

Barret, Don Carlos
1788-1838

Attorney, Law partner of E. M. Pease,
Early civic leader in Texas
Buried: Old Cemetery, Brazoria.

Barrow, Clyde Chesnut
1909-1934

Outlaw; First crime was auto theft in
1926; Met Bonnie Parker when he was
on parole in 1932; During the 2 years of
kidnapping and robbery they killed 12
people; Rescued Raymond Hamilton
from prison work gang; He and Bonnie
were shot by Texas Rangers near
Gibsland, Louisiana; taken to Arcadia
Buried: Western Heights Cemetery,
Dallas.

Barstow, Joshua
-1836

Veteran of the Battle of San Jacinto;
1st Regiment, Texas Volunteers,

Company B
Buried: Phelps Plantation, Orozimbo, Brazoria County.

Barton, Thomas B.
-1836

Massacred as one of Fannin's men at Goliad
Buried: Goliad.

Bass, Sam
1851-1878

Outlaw, Robbery career began in 1877; Held up many stage coaches and trains; Died of wound received while robbing bank at Round Rock
Buried: Round Rock, Texas.

Bates, Anthony
-1836

Massacred as one of Fannin's men at Goliad
Buried: Goliad.

Battle, Mills M.
1800-1856

Member of Austin's Old 300, Alcalde of San Felipe, Delegate to the Convention of 1836, County Clerk of Fort Bend County, Carpenter and contractor
Buried: Richmond, Texas.

Batts, James S.
-1836

Massacred as one of Fannin's men at Goliad
Buried: Golaid.

Baugh, John J.
1803-1836

Veteran of the Siege of Bexar; When Travis was killed in the Alamo, Baugh assumed command, Rank of captain; Killed in the Battle of the Alamo
Buried: with other heroes of the Alamo.

Bayless, Joseph
-1836

Perished defending the Alamo, March 6, 1836, at age of 28.

Baylor, George Wythe
1832-1916

Ardent secessionist, 1st to raise the Confederate flag in Austin, Veteran of the Battle of Shiloh and the Red River Campaign, Texas Ranger after the Civil War
Buried: Confederate Cemetery, San Antonio.

Baylor,
Robert Emmett Bledsoe
1793-1873

Lawyer,; Member of the United States Congress; Ordained Baptist minister in 1839; Assisted in the organization of Texas Baptist Education Society from which would develop Baylor University; Served as judge during the Republic; Member of the Convention of 1845; Ardent member of the Masonic Order; Organized courts and churches all over Texas; Author of the Charter of Baylor University; Law professor at Baylor; Trustee of Baylor
Buried: Campus of "Baylor College" (present Mary Hardin Baylor University), Belton.

Bays, Joseph
1786-1854

Member of Austin's Old 300, Friend of Daniel Boone, Baptist preacher who preached the first recorded Baptist service in Texas (near San Augustine, 1820)
Buried: Matagorda, Texas.

Beall, Josias B.
-1836

Massacred as one of Fannin's men at Goliad
Buried: Goliad.

Bean, Candace Midkiff
1802-1848

Wife of Peter Ellis Bean (Filibuster, member of Philip Nolan's expedition to Texas, East Texas settler, Buried in Jalapa, Mexico)
Buried: Selman Cemetery, Linwood.

Bean, Roy
1825-1903

After considerable activity in Mexico and California, Bean arrived in Texas during Civil War times. Drifted here and there until 1882, then set up tent saloons after railroad construction. Moved his headquarters from his saloon, "Vinegarroon", to Langtry and, in 1885, became justice of the peace at the request of Texas Ranger Oglesby. Became known as the "Law West of the Pecos"
Buried: Whitehead Museum, Del Rio.

Beard, Andrew Jackson
1814-1866

Veteran of the Battle of San Jacinto; 2nd Regiment, Texas Volunteers,

Infantry, 4th Company
Buried: Big Creek Cemetery, 20 miles S
of Richmond, Texas.

Beard, John
-1842

Killed at Dawson Massacre
Buried: Monument Hill, LaGrange.

Beck, John
-1836

Massacred as one of Fannin's men
at Goliad
Buried: Goliad.

Bee, Hamilton Prioleau
1822-1897

Confederate General from Texas,
Commander at Brownsville
Buried: San Antonio.

**Belknap,
William Goldsmith**
1794-1851

Veteran of War of 1812, Veteran of
Mexican War with distinguished
service record
Buried: Ft. Belknap.

Bell, James Madison
1817-1848

Veteran of San Jacinto; 1st Regiment,
Texas Volunteers, Company D
Buried: 8 miles east of Yorktown.

Bell, Josiah Hughes
1791-1838

Member of Austin's Old 300
Buried: Columbia.

Bell, Marvin
-1836

Massacred as one of Fannin's men
at Goliad
Buried: Goliad.

Bell, Peter Hansborough
1812-1898

Veteran of San Jacinto; 2nd Regiment,
Texas Volunteers, Company J, Cavalry;
Veteran of the Mexican War; Texas
Ranger with Jack C. Hays; Governor of
Texas (1849-1853); U. S. Senator
Buried: State Cemetery in Austin.

Bell, Thaddus Constantine
1822-1871

1st male baby born in Austin's colonies
Buried: Presbyterian Cemetery, West
Columbia.

Bellows, Fred J.
-1836

Massacred as one of Fannin's men
at Goliad
Buried: Goliad.

Bennett, Joseph L.
  -1843

Veteran of San Jacinto; 2nd Regiment Staff
Buried: Family Cemetery 3 miles from Streetman.

Bennett, Miles S.
1816-1849

Veteran of San Jacinto, "Soldier in Army of Texas 1836"
Buried: Pilgrim Cemetery southeast of Elkhart.

Bennett, Valentine
1780-1843

Veteran of Velasco, Veteran of Battle of Concepcion, Veteran of Battle of Bexar, Assistant Quartermaster of the Texas Army, Veteran of San Jacinto, Sent on the Santa Fe Expedition, Veteran of the Somervell Expedition
Buried: Gonzales.

Benson, Ellis
1808-1892

Veteran of Velasco, Veteran of San Jacinto (artillery)
Buried: Houston.

Bentley, Henry Hogue
  -1836

Massacred as one of Fannin's men at Goliad
Buried: Goliad.

Benton, Daniel
  -1841

Veteran of San Jacinto; Regular Infantry, Company A
Buried: Bexar County.

Berry, Andrew Jackson
1816-1899

Veteran of San Jacinto; 1st Regiment, Texas Volunteers, Company C; With Ed Burleson at Plum Creek; Veteran of Civil War
Buried: Belle Plain Cemetery near Baird.

Berry, David
  -1842

Killed at Dawson Massacre
Buried: Monument Hill, LaGrange.

Berry, John
  -1867

Gunsmith (repaired David Crockett's gun), Veteran of War of 1812
Buried: Berry Cemetery, Georgetown.

Berry, John Bate
  (son of John)

Veteran of the Battle of San Jacinto; Held rear guard at Harrisburg; Texas Ranger; Drew white bean on Meir Expedition; Veteran of the Mexican

War, Indian fighter
Buried: Bradbury Cemetery, Mason County.

Berry, Kearie Lee
1893-1965

Athlete and coach; Had a long and distinguished military career, Veteran of the Battle of Bataan and survivor of the Death March, Rank of General in U.S. Army
Buried: Fort Sam Houston National Cemetery, San Antonio.

Berryman, Helena Dill
1804-1888

First Anglo-American white child born in Texas to English speaking parents; One of the first contributors to Buckner Orphans Home
Buried: Forest Hills Plantation near Alto.

Besser, John S.
1802-1893

Drafted rules for the operation of State Prison at Huntsville
Buried: Huntsville.

Billingsley, Jesse
1810-1880

Veteran of the Battle of San Jacinto; 1st Regiment, Texas Volunteers, Company C; Texas Ranger; Congressman of the Republic; State Senator
Buried: State Cemetery, Austin.

Bingham, Benjamin Rice
-1836

Killed at the Battle of San Jacinto
Buried: on the field at San Jacinto.

Birdsall, Judge John
-1839

Attorney General of the Republic (1837-1838), Chief Justice of the Supreme Court (1838)
Buried: Glendale Cemetery, Houston.

Blackwell, Joseph H.
-1836

Massacred as one of Fannin's men at Goliad
Buried: Goliad.

Blackwell, Thomas H.
-1851

Veteran of the Battle of San Jacinto; 2nd Regiment, Texas Volunteers, Cavalry
Buried: at his home in Brazoria County.

Blair, John
-1836

Perished defending the Alamo, March 6, 1836, at age of 33.

Blair, Samuel
-1836

Perished defending the Alamo, March 6, 1836, at age of 29, Rank of captain.

Blake, Thomas M.
-1836

Massacred as one of Fannin's men at Goliad
Buried: Goliad.

Blakey, Lemuel Stockton
-1836

Killed at the Battle of San Jacinto
Buried: on the field at San Jacinto.

Blazeby, William
-1836

Perished defending the Alamo, March 6, 1836, at age of 41, Rank of captain.

Bledsoe, George L.
1805-1887

2nd Regiment, Texas Volunteers, 4th Company, Infantry
Buried: Honey Grove, Texas.

Bledsoe, Jules
1898-1943

Negro baritone, composer of many songs; Sang "Old Man River" in "Showboat" in 1924
Buried: Greenwood Cemetery, Waco.

Blocker, Abner Pickins
1856-1943

Drove cattle up the Texas trails for 17 years, Devised the XIT brand
Buried: Dignowitty Cemetery, San Antonio.

Blocker, Dan
1928-1972

Football star, TV personality; Played the character of Hoss Cartwright on "Bonanza" for 13 seasons; Co-owner of the Bonanza steak houses
Buried: Woodman Cemetery, DeKalb.

Blocker, John Rufus
1851-1927

With brother, Abner, drove cattle from Texas; Owner of ranches in Tom Green, Maverick and Dimmit Counties; 1st president of the Trail Drivers Association
Buried: Dignowitty Cemetery, San Antonio.

Blount, Stephen William
1808-1890

Signer of the Texas Declaration of Independence, From Georgia
Buried: San Augustine.

Boatright, Mody Coggin
1896-1970

Folklorist, One of the most illustrious names in Texas letters, Professor of English at UT for 43 years
Buried: Glenrest Cemetery, Kerrville.

Boggess, Lynwood (Dusty)
1904-1968

Member of Texas Sports Hall of Fame, Baseball, 19 years as an umpire
Buried: Hillcrest Cemetery, Dallas.

Booker, Shields (MD)
-1843

Veteran of San Jacinto; Assistant Surgeon, 2nd Regiment, Texas Volunteers; Killed at Perote Prison
Buried: his home in Brazoria County.

Bolton, William Thomas
1910-1976

Founder of Southwestern Historical Wax Museum (1962)
Buried: IOOF Cemetery, Denton.

Bonham, James Butler
1807-1836

Perished defending the Alamo, Rank of Lieutenant, age 29 years; Friend and former classmate of William B. Travis. Twice he slipped through the Mexican lines to go for help for the Alamo defenders. On March 3, he defied enemy fire to reenter the Alamo, where he died.

Bonner, Mary
-1935

"Texas girl etcher of cowboys"; Her etchings appear in museums around the world
Buried: Mission Burial Park, San Antonio.

Boone, Hannibal Honestus
1834-1897

Served with John S. Ford through the Civil War; Lawyer in Navasota
Buried: Navasota.

Borden, John P.
1812-1890

Veteran of Goliad when it was captured; Veteran of the Battle of San Jacinto; Brother of Gail Borden, Jr. (Borden Milk); Lawyer in Richmond; Last surviving officer of San Jacinto; 1st Regiment, Texas Volunteers, Company D
Buried: Weimar Cemetery, Richmond, Texas.

Borden, Paschal Pavolo
1806-1864

Veteran of the Battle of San Jacinto; 1st Regiment, Texas Volunteers,

Company D; Brother of Gail, Jr. and John
Buried: Seclusion near Egypt, Texas.

Bordon, Thomas Henry
1804-1877

One of Austin's Old 300; Inventor, Constructed first windmill on Galveston Island; Stephen F. Austin's official surveyor; Veteran of the Grass Fight and the Siege of Bexar; Brother of Gail, Jr., John and Paschal
Buried: Galveston.

Bostick, Sion Record
1818-1902

Veteran of the Siege of Bexar, the Battle of San Jacinto and the Plum Creek Fight; 1st Regiment, Texas Volunteers, Company D; Veteran of the Mexican War and Hood's Brigade
Buried: San Saba, Texas.

Bouch, Gabriel
-1836

Massacred as one of Fannin's men at Goliad
Buried: Goliad.

Bourne, Daniel
-1836

Perished defending the Alamo, March 6, 1836, at age of 26.

Bower, John White
1808-1902

Signer of the Texas Declaration of Independence, from Georgia; His daughter married the son of Empresario James Power
Buried: Bower Family Cemetery near Trivoli, Refugio County.

Bowers, John Henry (M.D.)
1817-1907

Served as Doctor of Texas Army with Dr. Ashbel Smith; Expert in treating yellow fever and cholera; Was en route to San Jacinto when the battle occurred
Buried: Odd Fellows Cemetery, Columbus.

Bowie, James
1795-1836

Perished defending the Alamo, March 6, 1836; Came to Texas to search for lost silver mine on the San Saba River in 1828; Texas Ranger; Lost his wife and two sons to cholera in 1833; Veteran of the Battle of Concepcion, of the Siege of Bexar; Rank of Colonel; Came down with typhoid and

pneumonia in the Alamo
Buried: Sarcaphagus in San Fernando Cathedral in San Antonio (with the other heroes of the Alamo).

Bowman, Jesse B.
-1836

Perished defending the Alamo, March 6, 1836.

Box, James Edward
1814-1851

2nd Regiment, 1st Company Infantry
Buried: Old Cemetery at Palestine.

Box, John Andrew
1803-1874

Veteran of the Battle of San Jacinto; 2nd Regiment, Texas Volunteers, 1st Company, Infantry
Buried: Box-Bessum Cemetery 3 miles S of Crockett.

Box, Nelson

Veteran of the Battle of San Jacinto; 2nd Regiment, Texas Volunteers, 1st Company
Buried: Box-Bessum Cemetery 3 miles S of Crockett.

Box, Thomas Griffin (Rev.)
1817-1859

Veteran of the Battle of San Jacinto; 2nd Regiment, Texas Volunteers, 1st Company
Buried: Box-Bessum Cemetery 3 miles S of Crockett.

Boynton, Benjamin Lee
1898-1963

Texas Sports Hall of Fame for Football; 1st Texan to be named to an All-American Team (from Williams College); Organized Southwest Conference Officials Association
Buried: Restland Abby, Dallas.

Bracey, Leslie G. H.
-1836

Massacred as one of Fannin's men at Goliad
Buried: Goliad.

Brackenridge, George Washington
1832-1920

Union sympathizer (brothers in CSA Army); Organized San Antonio National Bank; Regent of the University of Texas; Educational benefactor in San Antonio, Galveston (50 acres of land for UT); Gave land for parks in San Antonio
Buried: Brackenridge Cemetery, 8

miles SE of Edna, Jackson County.

Bradburn, Juan Davis

Kentucky native who escaped from Tennessee jail (in for stealing slaves); Sent by Mexican Government to Anahuac to carry out Law of 1830; Jailed Travis, Patrick Jack and Edwin Waller, Removed from command, Returned to Texas with Mexican Army in 1836
Buried: Mission, Texas.

Bradford, James A.
-1836

Massacred as one of Fannin's men at Goliad
Buried: Goliad.

Bradshaw, Wesley
1897-1960

Texas Sports Hall of Fame for Football
Buried: Greenwood Cemetery, Fort Worth

Brady, Leslie G.
-1836

Killed at Battle of Refugio in Texas Revolution
Buried: Mt. Calvary Cemetery, Refugio.

Branch, Edward Thomas
1811-1861

Veteran of the Battle of San Jacinto; 2nd Regiment, Texas Volunteers, 3rd Company, Infantry; Member of 1st and 2nd Congresses; Supreme Court Judge
Buried: Branch family cemetery 1 mile from Liberty, Texas.

Braniff, Thomas Elmer
1883-1954

One of nation's leading insurance men, Chairman and president of Prudential Insurance; In 1927 bought a second-hand airplane and established first airline in the Southwest (now Braniff International); Philanthropist
Buried: Calvary Cemetery, Dallas.

Brannon,
Byron Scott ("Buster")
1908-1979

Texas Sports Hall of Fame for Football
Buried: Greenwood Cemetery, Fort Worth.

Brashear, Richard G.
-1836

Massacred as one of Fannin's men at Goliad
Buried: Goliad.

Brewer, Henry Mitchell
1807-1849

Veteran of the Battle of San Jacinto; 2nd Regiment, Texas Volunteers, 1st Company, Infantry
Buried: Brewer family cemetery near Douglas, Nacogdoches County.

Brewer, J. Mason
1897-1975

Historian and recorder of folk tales; Professor of English at ETSU; Author of **The Word on the Brazos, Aunt Dicy Tales, Dog Ghosts and Other Texas Folk Tales**
Buried: Evergreen Cemetery, Austin.

Bridges, Frank
1890-1970

Texas Sports Hall of Fame for Football; Coach at Baylor University when school won its first Southwest Conference championship
Buried: San Antonio.

Briggs, Elisha Andrews
1820-1906

Texas Ranger with John Coffee (Jack) Hays and William A. A. (Bigfoot) Wallace; In 1874 entered the ministry and organized the Rio Grande Baptist Association at Frio Town
Buried: Frio.

Brigham, Asa
1790-1844

Signer of the Texas Declaration of Independence, from Massachusetts; Treasurer of the Republic, State Treasurer, Mayor of Austin
Buried: Washington State Park, Washington, Texas.

Brigham, Moses W.
-1854

Veteran of the Battle of San Jacinto; 1st Regiment, Texas Volunteers
Buried: Founders' Memorial Park, Houston.

**Bringhurst,
Antoinette Power Houston**
1852-1932

Well-known poet, Poet Laureate of the Daughters of the Republic of Texas, Daughter of Sam and Margaret Lea Houston
Buried: Mission Burial Park, San Antonio.

**Brinker,
Maureen Connolly**
1934-1969

Internationally famous tennis champion, Nicknamed "Little Mo"
Buried: Hillcrest, Dallas.

Briscoe, Andrew
1810-1849

Signer of the Texas Declaration of Independence, from Mississippi
Buried: State Cemetery, Austin.

Brister, Nathaniel
-1836

Massacred as one of Fannin's men at Goliad
Buried: Goliad.

Brodbeck, Jacob
1821-1909

Native of Germany; School teacher and superintendent; Experimented with a windless clock and an airplane with rudder, wings and propeller (1863); Much ahead of his time, he found no fiscal backing for his inventions; Farmed at Luckenback
Buried: Luckenback, Gillispie County.

Brookfield, Francis E.
-1842

Killed at the Dawson Massacre
Buried: Monument Hill, LaGrange.

Brooks, John Sowers
1814-1836

Was with Fannin and gave Goliad the title of Fort Defiance; Wounded an captured at Coleto; Executed as part of the Goliad Massacre
Buried: Goliad.

Brooks, Micajah Madison
1856-1934

Practiced law at Forney and Greenville; Drew charter for Southern Methodist University; 1st President of Board of Trustees of SMU
Buried: Greenville.

Brotherington, Robert

One of Austin's Old 300
Buried: Columbus.

Brown, George
-1844

Veteran of the Battle of San Jacinto; 1st Regiment, Texas Volunteers, Company B; Music-maker of San Jacinto
Buried: City Cemetery, Houston.

Brown, George
-1836

Perished defending the Alamo, March 6, 1836, at age of 35.

Brown, Herman
1892-1962

Founder of Brown and Root Construction Company (now a part of Halliburton)
Buried: Glenwood Cemetery, Houston.

Brown, James *-1836*	Perished defending the Alamo, March 6, 1836, at age of 36.
Brown, J. *-1836*	Massacred as one of Fannin's men at Goliad Buried: Goliad.
Brown, Oliver *-1836*	Massacred as one of Fannin's men at Goliad Buried: Goliad.
Brown, Oliver *-1836*	Massacred as one of Fannin's men at Goliad Buried: Goliad.
Brown, Robert *-1836*	Perished defending the Alamo, March 6, 1836.
Brown, Wilson C. *1810-1876*	2nd Regiment, Texas Volunteers, Company J. Cavalry Buried: Jasper.
Brown, William S. *-1836*	Massacred as one of Fannin's men at Goliad Buried: Goliad.
Browning, David Greig (Skippy) *1932-1956*	Texas Sports Hall of Fame for swimming and diving Buried: Restland, Dallas.
Browning, George Washington *1806-1879*	Veteran of San Jacinto; Regular Infantry Company; Lawyer Buried: Austin.
Bryan, Guy Morrison *1821-1901*	Carried Travis' letter (asking help for the Alamo defenders) to Brazoria and Velasco; Attended school of Thomas J. Pilgrim; Ranger under "Jack" Hays; Son of Emily Austin Bryan (Stephen F. Austin's sister) and stepson of James F. Perry, Brother of Moses Austin Bryan; Confederate soldier and a leader in the secessionist movement Buried: State Cemetery, Austin.
Bryan, John Neely *1810-1877*	Founder of the city of Dallas, Early Texas settler Buried: Paupers Graveyard, Austin.

Bryan, Luke O.
1807-1869

Veteran of the Battle of San Jacinto; 2nd Regiment, Texas Volunteers, 3rd Company
Buried: Bryan family cemetery near Liberty.

Bryan, Moses Austin
1817-1895

Veteran of the Battle of San Jacinto; 1st Regiment, Texas Volunteers, Company D; Aide-de-camp to General Rusk; Interpreter for Sam Houston and Santa Anna at San Jacinto; Confederate Veteran; Nephew of Stephen F. Austin and brother of Guy M. Bryan
Buried: Independence.

Bryan, William Joel
1815-1903

Veteran of the Siege of Bexar; Member of the Texas Army but ill at time of Battle of San Jacinto; Nephew of Stephen Austin and brother of Moses and Guy Bryan
Buried: Peach Point.

Bryant,
Benjamin Franklin
1800-1857

Veteran of the Battle of San Jacinto; 2nd Regiment, Texas Volunteers, 7th Company, Infantry; Built fort called Bryant Station on Little River and protected it against Indians
Buried: State Cemetery, Austin.

Bryson, John M.
-1836

Massacred as one of Fannin's men at Goliad
Buried: Goliad.

Buchanan, James
-1836

Perished defending the Alamo, March 6, 1836, at age of 23.

Buck,
Beaumont Bonaparte
1860-1950

West Point graduate; Served at Fort McIntosh, Fort Ringgold, Fort Sherman; During World War I won DSC, Medal of the French Legion of Honor, Croix de Guerre; Promoted to rank of general
Buried: Fort Sam Houston National Cemetery, San Antonio.

Buck, Frank
1884-1950

Wild game trapper and trainer; Slogan was "Bring 'em back alive." Author, world traveler; 1st expedition to South

America in 1911
Cremated and ashes scattered over mountain area close to San Angelo.

Buckley, Daniel
-1836

Massacred as one of Fannin's men at Goliad
Buried: Goliad.

Buckner, Robert Cooke
1833-1919

Baptist Minister, Established Buckner Orphans' Home in 1879
Buried: Grove Hill, Dallas.

Buffington, Anderson
1806-1891

Veteran of San Jacinto; 2nd Regiment, Texas Volunteers, 8th Company, Infantry; Baptist Minister, County Judge
Buried: Odd Fellows Cemetery, Anderson.

Buford, Thomas Young
1814-1839

Soldier in the Texas Army
Buried: Oak Grove Cemetery, Nacogdoches.

Bunton, John Wheeler
1807-1879

Veteran of Siege of Bexar and of San Jacinto; 1st Regiment, Texas Volunteers, Company C; Signer of the Texas Declaration of Independence
Buried: State Cemetery, Austin.

Burbidge, Thomas
-1836

Massacred as one of Fannin's men at Goliad
Buried: Goliad.

Burch, James
1806-1873

2nd Regiment, Texas Volunteers, 8th Company, Infantry
Buried: Catholic Cemetery, Colita.

Burch, Valentine
1804-1895

2nd Regiment, Texas Volunteers, 8th Company, Infantry
Buried: Peach Tree Village, Polk County.

Burleson, Aaron B.
1815-1885

Veteran of the Siege of Bexar and the Battle of San Jacinto; 1st Regiment, Texas Volunteers, Company C; With group that captured Santa Anna; Brother of Edward Burleson

Burleson, Albert Sidney
1863-1937

Buried: Burleson family cemetery, Kyle.

Lawyer, Postmaster General of the U. S. under Woodrow Wilson; Was responsible for inaugurating the first ail mail system in the world, May 15, 1918
Buried: Oakwood Cemetery, Austin.

Burleson, Edward
1798-1851

Veteran of the Battle of San Jacinto; 1st Regiment, Texas Volunteers, Infantry (commander of group); Congressman during Republic; Laid out town of Waterloo (present day Austin); Vice-President of the Republic
Buried: State Cemetery, Austin (1st person to be buried there — 1851).

Burleson, Rufus Columbus
1823-1901

Baptist minister who volunteered for missionary work in Texas; 2nd president of Baylor at Independence; Baptized Sam Houston (Nov. 19, 1854); 1st president of Baylor in Waco
Buried: Oakwood Cemetery, Waco.

Burnet, David Gouverneur
1788-1870

1st American to volunteer with Franciso de Miranda's attempt to free Venezuela from Spain; lived with the Comanches for 2 years; An empresario; President of Ad Interium government; President of the Republic
Buried: State Cemetery, Austin.

Burnett, Samuel Burk
1849-1922

Cattleman and trail boss, Owner of the 6666 Ranch
Buried: Fort Worth.

Burns, Samuel E.
-1836

Perished defending the Alamo, March 6, 1836, at age of 26.

Burt, Benjamin F.
-1836

Massacred as one of Fannin's men at Goliad
Buried: Goliad.

Burton, Isaac Watts
1805-1843

Veteran of the Battle of San Jacinto; 2nd Regiment, Texas Volunteers, Cavalry; Only San Jacinto veteran who

had attended West Point; Congressman during the Republic; Lawyer in Nacogdoches
Buried: Glenwood Cemetery, Crockett.

Bust, Luke W.

1st Regiment, Texas Volunteers, Company A; Died at Velasco after the battle
Buried: Velasco, Texas.

Butler, George D.
-1836

Perished defending the Alamo, March 6, 1836, at age of 23.

Butler, Moses
-1836

Massacred as one of Fannin's men at Goliad
Buried: Goliad.

Butler, Thomas J.
-1842

Killed at the Dawson Massacre
Buried: Monument Hill, LaGrange.

Byars, Noah Turner
1808-1888

Armorer for Sam Houston; The Convention of 1836 was held in his blacksmith shop; founder of 1st Baptist Church, Waco, numerous other churches and 2 academies
Buried: Brownwood.

Bynum, Alfred
-1836

Massacred as one of Fannin's men at Goliad
Buried: Goliad.

Byrne, Mathew
-1836

Massacred as one of Fannin's men at Goliad
Buried: Goliad.

Byrom,
John Smith Davenport
1798-1837

Veteran of the Battle of Velasco, Signer of the Texas Declaration of Independence, from Georgia
Buried: Presbyterian Cemetery, West Columbia.

Caddell, Andrew
1795-1869

Veteran of the Battle of San Jacinto; 2nd Regiment, Texas Volunteers, 8th Company (Capt. William Kimbro's company)
Buried: Three Forks Cemetery, 3 miles SE of Belton.

Cage, Benjamin Franklin
-1838

Veteran of the Battle of San Jacinto; 2nd Regiment, Texas Volunteers, 4th Company, Infantry
Buried: Old Catholic Cemetery near Milam Square, San Antonio.

Cain, J. W.
-1836

Massacred as one of Fannin's men at Goliad
Buried: Goliad.

Calder, Robert James
1810-1885

Veteran of the Battle of San Jacinto; 1st Regiment, Texas Volunteers, Company K
Buried: Richmond, Texas.

Caldwell, Mathew
1798-1842

The "Paul Revere of Texas." Signer of the Texas Declaration of Independence, from Kentucky
Buried: Oak Grove Cemetery, Nacogdoches.

Callahan, James Hughes
1814-1856

Veteran of Battle of Coleto, captured, escaped Goliad Massacre; Texas Ranger
Buried: State Cemetery, Austin.

Callahan, Thomas Jefferson
1817-1880

Veteran of the Battle of San Jacinto; Regular Infantry, Company B
Buried: Wharton family cemetery near Clute.

Callison, James Henry
-1836

Killed at the Battle of Refugio in the Texas Revolution
Buried: Mt. Calvary Cemetery, Refugio.

Calvit, Alexander
1784-1836

Member of Austin's Old 300
Buried: Bells Landing family cemetery, Brazoria County.

Cameron, William Waldo
1879-1939

Founder of William Cameron and Co. (lumber and hardware businesses)
Buried: Waco.

Campbell, Robert
-1836

Perished defending the Alamo, March 6, 1836, rank of lieutenant.

Campbell, Thomas Mitchell
1836-1923

Governor of Texas (1907-1911); Prison system reformed; Pure food laws passed
Buried: East Hill Cemetery, Palestine.

Cane, John *-1836*	Perished defending the Alamo; One of 32 from Gonzales who went to the defense of the Alamo, Age 34 Buried: with Alamo heroes.
Cannon, William Jarvis *1808-1881*	Veteran of the Battle of San Jacinto; 1st Regiment, Texas Volunteers, Company H Buried: Oyster Creek, 4 miles from Velasco.
Carabajel, Mariano *-1836*	Massacred as one of Fannin's men at Goliad Buried: Goliad.
Carey, William R. *-1836*	Perished defending the Alamo, March 6, 1836; Rank of captain, at age of 30.
Carlisle, **George Washington** *-1836*	Massacred as one of Fannin's men at Goliad Buried: Goliad.
Carrier, Charles J. *-1836*	Massacred as one of Fannin's men at Goliad Buried: Goliad.
Carroll, Benajah Harvey *1843-1914*	Early Baptist minister and leader Buried: Oakwood Cemetery, Waco.
Carroll, Horace Bailey *1903-1966*	Historian, Associate Director of the Texas Historical Association, Editor of "Southwest Historical Quarterly", Co-Editor of **The Handbook of Texas** Buried: Gatesville, Texas.
Carroll, Michael E. *-1836*	Massacred as one of Fannin's men at Goliad Buried: Goliad.
Carter, Amon Giles *1879-1955*	Owner of the **Fort Worth Star Telegram**; Important developer of Fort Worth, Philanthropist Buried: Fort Worth.
Cartwright, Mathew W. *1813-1884*	Veteran of the Battle of San Jacinto; 2nd Regiment, Texas Volunteers, 2nd Company

Cartwright, William
1813-1844

Buried: Cartwright family cemetery, 1 mile NE of Keenan, Texas.

Veteran of the Battle of San Jacinto; 2nd Regiment, Texas Volunteers, 2nd Company
Buried: Cartwright family cemetery 1 mile NE of Keenan, Texas.

Caruth, William
1827-1885

Early settler of Dallas County
Buried: Hillcrest, Dallas.

Caruthers, Allen
1804-1863

Veteran of the Battle of San Jacinto; 1st Regiment, Texas Volunteers, Company H
Buried: Cemetery 8 miles SW of Clinton, Texas.

Caruthers, Ewing
-1836

Massacred as one of Fannin's men at Goliad
Buried: Goliad.

Cash, George W.
-1836

Massacred as one of Fannin's men at Goliad
Buried: Goliad.

Cash, John L.
-1843

Victim of the Mier Expedition
Buried: Monument Hill, LaGrange.

**Castaneda,
Carlos Eduardo**
1896-1958

Eminent Historian, Author of **Our Catholic Heritage in Texas**, Writer and Lecturer
Buried: Mt. Calvary Cemetery, Austin.

Castrillion, Manuel F.
-1836

Major General in the Mexican Army under Santa Anna at Siege of the Alamo and the Battle of San Jacinto; Mortally wounded at San Jacinto
Buried: San Jacinto.

Cawthon, Pete
1898-1962

Texas Sports Hall of Fame for Football, Coach
Buried: Mexia.

Caylor, Harvey Wallace
1867-1932

Nationally recognized artist, Painter of Western scenes
Buried: Big Spring.

31

Chadwick, Joseph M.
  -1836

Massacred as one of Fannin's men at Goliad
Buried: Goliad.

Chamberland, Willard

1st Regiment, Texas Volunteers, Company H
Buried: on farm near Hico.

**Chambers,
Thomas Jefferson**
1802-1865

State Attorney for Coahuila and Texas (1834), Active part in events leading to Revolution
Buried: Episcopal Cemetery, Galveston.

**Chandor,
Douglas Granville**
1897-1953

Internationally known portrait artist, Originator of Chandor's Gardens near Weatherford
Buried: Greenwood Cemetery, Weatherford.

Cheevers, John
  -1846

Veteran of the Battle of San Jacinto; 2nd Regiment, Texas Volunteers, 5th Company, Infantry (Thomas McIntire's Company)
Buried: Founders' Memorial Park, Houston.

Cherry, Emma Richardson
1859-1954

Nationally known artist
Buried: Houston.

Cherry, Johnson Blair
1901-1966

Texas Sports Hall of Fame for Football; Coach at University of Texas, First coach to adopt "T" formation there
Buried: Llano Cemetery, Amarillo.

Chew, John
  -1836

Massacred as one of Fannin's men at Goliad
Buried: Goliad.

**Childress,
George Campbell**
1804-1841

Author of the Texas Declaration of Independence, from Tennessee
Buried: State Cemetery, Austin.

Chiles, Lewis L.
1811-1864

Veteran of the Battle of San Jacinto; 2nd Regiment, Texas Volunteers, 4th Company, Infantry
Buried: Old Cemetery, Caldwell.

Chilton, Horace
1853-1932

U. S. Senator — 1st native Texan to be elected to that office
Buried: Tyler.

Chisum, Enoch P. Gains
-1836

Massacred as one of Fannin's men at Goliad
Buried: Goliad.

Chisum, John Simpson
1824-1884

Rancher, Beef contractor for the Confederate Army; Herded cattle over many trails but not to extent of Loving, Goodnight, or Slaughter
Buried: Paris, Texas.

Church, John
-1842

Killed at the Dawson Massacre
Buried: Monument Hill, LaGrange.

Churchill, Thomas
-1836

Massacred as one of Fannin's men at Goliad
Buried: Goliad.

Clapp, Elisha
-1856

2nd Regiment, Texas Volunteers, Company J, Cavalry
Buried: Family cemetery 9 miles SW of Crockett.

Clark, Addison
1842-1911

Early well-known preacher, Disciples of Christ; 1st President of Add-Ran College, Fort Worth
Buried: Granbury.

Clark, Charles H.
-1836

Perished defending the Alamo, March 6, 1836.

Clark, Edward
1815-1880

Governor of Texas (March, 1861-November, 1861.) Hero, Battle of Mansfield.
Buried: Marshall

Clark, Joseph H.
-1836

Massacred as one of Fannin's men at Goliad
Buried: Goliad.

Clark, Seth
-1836

Massacred as one of Fannin's men at Goliad
Buried: Goliad.

Clark, William, Jr.
1798-1859

Signer of the Texas Declaration of Independence, from North Carolina
Buried: Oak Grove Cemetery, Nacogdoches.

Clayton, Joseph Alvey
1817-1873

Veteran of the Battle of San Jacinto, Artillery
Buried: Chatfield Cemetery, Navarro County.

Clements, Lewis C.
1816-1892

1st Regiment, Texas Volunteers, Company H
Buried: Brenham.

Clopper, Andrew M.
1791-1853

2nd Regiment, Texas Volunteers, Company J, Cavalry
Buried: Old Morris Cemetery, Seabrook, Harris County.

Cloud, Daniel William
-1836

Perished defending the Alamo, March 6, 1836, at age 22.

Cloud, John Wurts
1797-1850

Early Episcopal preacher, 1st ordained minister of the Episcopal Church in Texas
Buried: Washington-on-the-Brazos.

Cochran, Robert
-1836

Perished defending the Alamo, March 6, 1836, at age 26.

Cocke, James Decatur
-1842

Drew black bean (Mier Expedition) and was executed
Buried: Monument Hill, LaGrange.

Coe, John G.
-1836

Massacred as one of Fannin's men at Goliad
Buried: Goliad.

Coglan, George
-1836

Massacred as one of Fannin's men at Goliad
Buried: Goliad.

Coke, Richard
1829-1897

Governor of Texas (1874-1876), Texas A&M provided for during his term; U.S. Senator
Buried: Oakwood Cemetery, Waco.

Cole, William H.
-1836

Massacred as one of Fannin's men at Goliad
Buried: Goliad.

Colegrove, John H.
-1836

Killed at the Battle of Refugio in The Texas Revolution
Buried: Mt. Calvary Cemetery, Refugio.

Coleman, Jacob
-1836

Massacred as one of Fannin's men at Goliad
Buried: Goliad.

Coleman, Robert Morris
1799-1837

On Houston's staff at San Jacinto; Signer of the Texas Declaration of Independence, from Kentucky; Texas Ranger; Drowned in the Brazos River near Velasco
Buried: Velasco.

Coles, John P.
1793-1847

Member of Austin's Old 300
Buried: Independence (Quadrangle area).

Collar, Job S.
-1867

Veteran of the Battle of San Jacinto; 2nd Regiment, 2nd Company
Buried: Madisonville.

**Collins,
Harry Warren (Rip)**
1896-1968

One of the greatest athletes in Texas History; Hero of Texas A&M; New York Yankee pitcher (108-82 in 11 seasons), Texas Ranger
Buried: Bryan.

Collingsworth, James
1806-1838

Signer of the Texas Declaration of Independence, from Tennessee; Veteran of the Battle of San Jacinto; Houston's aide-de-camp; Attorney General of the Republic
Buried: Founders' Memorial Park, Houston.

Colquitt, Oscar Branch
1861-1940

Governor of Texas (1911-1915); Programs included 8-hour work day, workmen's compensation, child labor laws and penal reform
Buried: Oakwood Cemetery, Austin.

Colston, William John
-1836

Massacred as one of Fannin's men at Goliad
Buried: Goliad.

Comstock, William
-1836

Massacred as one of Fannin's men at Goliad
Buried: Goliad.

Conlee, Preston
1798-1874

Veteran of the Battle of San Jacinto; 1st Regiment, Texas Volunteers, Company C
Buried: Fairview Cemetery, Gainesville.

Conley, John (Snipe)
1892-1978

Texas Sports Hall of Fame for Baseball
Buried: DeSoto.

Connally, Thomas Terry
1877-1963

Veteran of the Spanish-American War, U. S. Congressman and Senator from Texas
Buried: Marlin.

Conrad, Cullen
-1836

Massacred as one of Fannin's men at Goliad
Buried: Goliad.

Conrad, Edward
1811-1836

Signer of the Texas Declaration of Independence, from Pennsylvania
Buried: Evergreen Cemetery, Victoria.

Conway, Mathew
-1836

Massacred as one of Fannin's men at Goliad
Buried: Goliad.

Cook, Thomas
-1836

Killed at the Battle of Refugio in the Texas Revolution
Buried: Mt. Calvary Cemetery, Refugio.

Cooke, Francis Jarvis
1816-1903

Veteran of the Battle of San Jacinto; 1st Regiment, Texas Volunteers, Company K
Buried: Salem Cemetery near Howth, Waller County.

Cooke, William G.
1808-1847

On Houston's staff at San Jacinto, Assistant Inspector General, Indian fighter, Veteran of the Council House

fight
Buried: Seguin.

Cooper, Mathias
-1836

Killed at the Battle of San Jacinto
Buried: On the field at San Jacinto.

Coppini, Pompeo
1870-1957

Nationally known sculptor; Sculptured the Alamo Cenotaph, busts of many famous Texans, Confederates and other Americans
Buried: Sunset Memorial Park, San Antonio.

Cosky, Thomas H.
-1836

Massacred as one of Fannin's men at Goliad
Buried: Goliad.

Cottle, George Washington
-1836

Perished defending the Alamo, One of 32 from Gonzales who went to the defense of the Alamo, Age of 38
Buried: With the heroes of the Alamo.

Courtman, Henry
-1836

Perished defending the Alamo, March 6, 1836, at age of 28.

Cowan, William J.
-1836

Massacred as one of Fannin's men at Goliad
Buried: Goliad.

Cox, Harvey
-1836

Massacred as one of Fannin's men at Goliad
Buried: Goliad.

Cozart, Henderson
-1836

Massacred as one of Fannin's men at Goliad
Buried: Goliad.

Craddock, John Robert
1812-1891

Veteran of the Battle of San Jacinto; 1st Regiment, Texas Volunteers, Company H
Buried: Family cemetery near Rogers, Bell County.

Crane, Martin McNulty
1855-1943

Eminent jurist and civic hero, Advocate of progressive democracy, For anti-trust laws, Chief counsel against Jim Ferguson during impreachment
Buried: Grove Hill Cemetery, Dallas.

Crane, William Carey
1816-1885

Baptist minister; President of Baylor University for 22 years; 1st president of Texas State Teachers Association; Chaired the committee which founded Sam Houston State Teachers College
Buried: State Cemetery, Austin.

Crawford, Lemuel
-1836

Perished defending the Alamo, March 6, 1836, at age of 22.

Crawford, Robert (Rev.)
1815-1888

Veteran of the Battle of San Jacinto; 1st Regiment, Texas Volunteers, Company K
Buried: Mt. Vernon Cemetery, Mt. Vernon, Texas.

Crawford, William Carrol
1804-1895

The last surviving signer of the Texas Declaration of Independence, from North Carolina
Buried: State Cemetery, Austin.

Criswell, William Vanoy
1815-1858

Veteran of the Battle of San Jacinto; 1st Regiment, Texas Volunteers, Company C
Buried: State Cemetery, Austin.

Crockett, David
1786-1836

Perished defending the Alamo, March 6, 1836. Served in the Tennessee Legislature and U. S. Congress (from Tennessee); Came to Texas when he "fell out" with Andrew Jackson. First wife was a descendant of Macbeth, King of Scotland. He was 50 when he died at the Alamo
Buried: With the other heroes of the Alamo.

Crockett, Elizabeth Patton
1788-1860

2nd wife of David Crockett
Buried: Acton, Texas.

Cross, John
-1836

Massacred as one of Fannin's men at Goliad
Buried: Goliad.

Crossman, Robert
-1836

Perished defending the Alamo, March 6, 1836, at age of 26.

Culberson, Charles Allen
1855-1925

Governor of Texas (1895-1899), Strict law enforcement, Arbitration laws, Economy in government; Served as U. S. Senator
Buried: East Oakwood Cemetery, Fort Worth.

Cummings, David P.
-1836

Perished defending the Alamo, March 6, 1836, at age of 27.

Cummings, George W.
-1836

Massacred as one of Fannin's men at Goliad
Buried: Goliad.

Cummings, John
-1842

Killed at the Dawson Massacre
Buried: Monument Hill, LaGrange.

Cummins, David P.
-1836

Perished defending the Alamo; One of 32 from Gonzales who went to the defense of the Alamo, at age of 27.
Buried: With the heroes of the Alamo.

Cunningham, John D.
-1836

Massacred as one of Fannin's men at Goliad
Buried: Goliad.

Cunningham, Leander Calvin
1810-1896

Veteran of the Battle of San Jacinto; 1st Regiment, Texas Volunteers, Company C
Buried: Waelder, Texas.

Cunningham, Minnie Fisher
1882-1964

Leader in Women's Suffrage in Texas
Buried: New Waverly.

Cunningham, Robert
-1836

Perished defending the Alamo, March 6, 1836, at age of 27.

Cureton, J. J. (Jack)
1826-1881

Indian fighter, Killed Chief Peta Nocona
Buried: near Palo Pinto.

Curtman, George F.
-1836

Massacred as one of Fannin's men at Goliad
Buried: Goliad.

Dale, Elijah Valentine
1807-1890

Veteran of the Battle of San Jacinto; 1st Regiment, Texas Volunteers,

	Company A Buried: San Geronimo Cemetery, Seguin.
Dallas, Walter R. *-1847*	Veteran of the Battle of San Jacinto 1st Regiment, Texas Volunteers, Company H; Nephew of George M. Dallas Buried: Near town of William Penn, Washington County.
Damon, Squire *-1836*	Perished defending the Alamo; One of 32 from Gonzales who went to the defense of the Alamo, at age 28 Buried: With the heroes of the Alamo.
Dancer, John *-1842*	Killed at the Dawson Massacre Buried: Monument Hill, LaGrange.
Dangers, Gottlieb Burchard *1811-1869*	Early Evangelical Protestant minister at Indianola, New Braunfels and Fredricksburg Buried: Fredricksburg.
Daniell, George Washington *-1836*	Massacred as one of Fannin's men at Goliad Buried: Goliad.
Darst, Edmund Calloway *1815-1838*	Veteran of the Battle of San Jacinto; 2nd Regiment, Texas Volunteers, 4th Company, Infantry Buried: near Damon, Brazoria County.
Darst, Jacob C. *-1836*	Perished defending the Alamo, One of 32 from Gonzales who went to the defense of the Alamo, at age of 48 Buried: With the heroes of the Alamo.
Dasher, Thomas Jefferson *-1836*	Massacred as one of Fannin's men at Goliad Buried: Goliad.
Davidson, Robert T. *-1836*	Massacred as one of Fannin's men at Goliad Buried: Goliad.

Davidson, Thomas Whitfield
1876-1974

Politician and Federal Judge, Oldest Federal Judge at the time of his retirement (89 years old)
Buried: Diana, Upshur County.

Davis, Edmund Jackson
1827-1883

Governor of Texas (1870-1874), Radical Reconstructionist
Buried: State Cemetery, Austin.

Davis, Fields
-1836

Killed at Battle of Refugio in Texas Revolution
Buried: Mt. Calvary Cemetery, Refugio.

Davis, George A.
-1836

Massacred as one of Fannin's men at Goliad
Buried: Goliad.

Davis, Jackson
-1836

Killed at Battle of Refugio in Texas Revolution
Buried: Mt. Calvary Cemetery, Refugio.

Davis, John
-1836

Perished defending the Alamo, March 6, 1836, age of 25.

Davis, Jesse Kencheloe
1802-1870

Veteran of the Battle of San Jacinto 2nd Regiment, Texas Volunteers, 4th Company, Infantry
Buried: Masonic Cemetery, Gonzales.

Davis, John
-1836

Perished defending the Alamo; One of 32 from Gonzales who went to the defense of the Alamo, age 25
Buried: with the heroes of the Alamo.

Davis, Walter W.
-1836

Massacred as one of Fannin's men at Goliad
Buried: Goliad.

Dawson, Nicholas Mosby
1808-1842

Veteran of San Jacinto; Military leader killed with his men at Battle of Salado, Sept. 18, 1842 (Mier Expedition)
Buried: Monument Hill, LaGrange.

Day, Freeman H. K.
-1836

Perished defending the Alamo, March 6, 1836, age of 30.

Day, H. B.
-1836

Massacred as one of Fannin's men at Goliad
Buried: Goliad.

Day, Jerry C.
-1836

Perished defending the Alamo, March 6, 1836, at age of 20.

**Dealey,
Edward Musgrove (Ted)**
1892-1969

President, then Chairman of the board of the A. H. Belo Corporation (1940-1968), Publisher of **The Dallas Morning News**
Buried: Grove Hill Cemetery, Dallas.

**Dealey,
George Bannerman**
1859-1946

President of the A. H. Belo Corporation (1920-1946), "Dean of American Journalists", A founder and president of the Dallas Historical Society
Buried: Grove Hill Cemetery, Dallas.

Dearduff, William
-1836

Perished defending the Alamo; One of 32 from Gonzales who went to the defense of the Alamo
Buried: with the heroes of the Alamo.

Debicki, Napoleon
-1836

Massacred as one of Fannin's men at Goliad
Buried: Goliad.

Dedrick, George
-1836

Massacred as one of Fannin's men at Goliad
Buried: Goliad.

De Golyer, Everett Lee
1886-1956

Geologist and oilman, With H. C. Karcher and Eugene McDermott, founder of Geophysical Services, Inc., Philanthropist
Buried: Sparkman-Hillcrest, Dallas.

De Leon, Martin
1765-1833

Empresario, Founder of the city of Victoria
Buried: Evergreen Cemetery, Victoria.

De Morse, Charles
1816-1887

Father of Texas Journalism; Editor publisher, statesman, soldier, lawyer, merchant, farmer; Father of Texas Democratic Party Press
Buried: Clarksville.

Denison, Stephen
-1836

Perished defending the Alamo, March 6, 1836, at age of 24.

Dennis, Joseph
-1836

Massacred as one of Fannin's men at Goliad
Buried: Goliad.

Dennis, Thomas Mason
1807-1877

Veteran of the Battle of San Jacinto 1st Regiment, Texas Volunteers, Company C
Buried: Rockport.

De Spain, Randolph
-1836

Massacred as one of Fannin's men at Goliad
Buried: Goliad.

Despallier, Charles
-1836

Perished defending the Alamo, One of 32 from Gonzales who went to the defense of the Alamo, Age 24
Buried: with the heroes of the Alamo.

Devereux Julien Sidney
1805-1856

Successful planter of East Texas; Representative to the Texas Legislature; His plantation, Monte Verdi, was a showplace of the state
Buried: Glenfawn, 20 miles south of Henderson, Rusk County.

Deveraux, Michael
-1836

Massacred as one of Fannin's men at Goliad
Buried: Goliad.

De Vore, Cornelius
1819-1884

Veteran of San Jacinto; 2nd Regiment, Texas Volunteers, 3rd Company, Infantry
Buried: Liberty Cemetery, Liberty.

De Witt, Evaline

Daughter of Sarah Seely DeWitt; Fashioned the "Come and Take It" flag used at Battle of Gonzales
Buried: 2.5 miles south of Gonzales.

De Witt, Green C.
1787-1835

Empresario, Founder of the city of Gonzales, Designer of the "Come and Take It" flag
Buried: Seeley League Cemetery, 1 mile SE of Gonzales.

De Witt, Sarah Seely
1789-1854

Wife of Green DeWitt; With her daughter, Evaline, made the "Come And Take It" flag
Buried: Seeley League Cemetery, 1 mile SE of Gonzales.

Dickerman, William P.
-1836

Massacred as one of Fannin's men at Goliad
Buried: Goliad.

Dickerson, L. W.
-1842

Killed at the Dawson Massacre
Buried: Monument Hill, LaGrange.

Dickinson, Almaron
-1836

Perished defending the Alamo, March 6, 1836; Blacksmith; Came to Texas in 1825; Captain of artillery at the Alamo where he died, at age of 26
Buried: with the heroes of the Alamo.

Dickinson, Angelina

Child of Almaron; "Babe of the Alamo"; Was in the Alamo during the siege, 15 months old
Buried: Galveston.

Dickinson, Noah, Jr.
-1836

Massacred as one of Fannin's men at Goliad
Buried: Goliad.

Dickinson, Suzanna
1815-1883

Wife of Alamaron Dickinson; Suzanna and their daughter, Angelina, were spared in the Battle of the Alamo; Married John W. Hannig in 1857
Buried: Oakwood Cemetery, Austin.

Dickson, Abishai
-1836

Massacred as one of Fannin's men at Goliad
Buried: Goliad.

Dickson, Henry H.
-1836

Massacred as one of Fannin's men at Goliad
Buried: Goliad.

Dies, Martin
1901-1972

Congressman from Texas for over 20 years; Concerned with subversives in the U. S.; Fought against all foreign aid
Buried: Garden of Memories Chapel, Lufkin.

Dieterich, Francis
1815-1860

Hero of the Texas Revolution fighting under Ward and Fannin; Escaped the Goliad Massacre
Buried: Oakwood Cemetery, Austin.

Dillard, James H.
-1836

Perished defending the Alamo, March 6, 1836, at age of 31.

Dimkins, James
-1836

Perished defending the Alamo, March 6, 1836.

Disch, Billy
1874-1953

Texas Sports Hall of Fame for Baseball, Coach
Buried: Austin.

Disney, Richard
-1836

Massacred as one of Fannin's men at Goliad
Buried: Goliad.

Dobie, James Frank
1888-1964

National literary figure, Writer of Texas Folklore, Professor of English at University of Texas for many years
Buried: State Cemetery, Austin.

Donoho, John
-1836

Massacred as one of Fannin's men at Goliad
Buried: Goliad.

Douglas, Henry L.
-1836

Massacred as one of Fannin's men at Goliad
Buried: Goliad.

Douglas, Kelsey
-1840

Participant in the Fredonia Rebellion of 1835, Veteran of Texas Revolution; Drove out marauding Cherokees from Nacogdoches; Town of Douglas named for him
Buried: Memorial Cemetery, Nacogdoches.

Douglas, William G.
-1836

Massacred as one of Fannin's men at Goliad
Buried: Goliad.

Dover, Sherod J.
-1836

Perished defending the Alamo, March 6, 1836, at age of 30.

Dowling,
Richard W. (Lt. Dick)
1838-1867

Red-haired Irish bartender; Won the Battle of Sabine Pass (Civil War), Organized Texas' 1st oil company (May 17, 1866) and Texas' 1st Savings and Loan
Buried: St. Vincent's Cemetery, Houston.

Downman, Henry M.
-1836

Massacred as one of Fannin's men at Goliad
Buried: Goliad.

Dreyfuss, Sol
1885-1951

With his father, Gerard, founded Dreyfuss and Son Department Store, Life member of the Texas Historical Association, Owner of the Dallas Baseball Club (1928)
Buried: Emanuel Cemetery, Dallas.

Driscoll, Clara (Sevier)
1881-1945

Granddaughter of Daniel O'Driscoll, President of the Daughters of the Republic of Texas, Instrumental in saving the Alamo as an historic shrine
Buried: City Cemetery N1, San Antonio.

Dubose,
William Perry Brown
-1836

Massacred as one of Fannin's men at Goliad
Buried: Goliad.

Duel, Lewis
-1836

Perished defending the Alamo, March 6, 1836, at age of 24.

Duffield, J. E.
-1836

Massacred as one of Fannin's men at Goliad
Buried: Goliad.

Dugan, David
-1840

Early Texas Settler, Sworn hater of Indians
Buried: 5 miles N of Bells.

Duke, Cordia Sloan
1877-1966

Ranch wife who became 1st female game warden in Texas
Buried: Dalhart.

Duke, Thomas Marshall
-1867

Member of Austin's Old 300
Buried: Hynes Bay Ranch, Refugio County.

Dunbar, William
1818-1881

Veteran of the Battle of San Jacinto;
1st Regiment, Texas Volunteers,
Company B
Buried: Catholic Cemetery, Galveston.

Duncan, James W.
-1836

Massacred as one of Fannin's men
at Goliad
Buried: Goliad.

Duncan, John
1788-1878

Veteran of the Battle of San Jacinto
1st Regiment, Texas Volunteers,
Company D
Buried: Duncan Family Cemetery near
Pledger, Matagorda County.

Dunham, Robert Holmes
-1843

Victim of the Mier Expedition
Buried: Monument Hill, LaGrange.

Dupre, Marcy Mathias
1866-1925

Early advocate of the Texas Inter-
scholastic league
Buried: Lubbock.

Durham, William Daniel
1815-1838

Veteran of the Siege of Bexar and of
San Jacinto
Buried: Old Founders Cemetery,
Houston.

Dusangue, Francis J.
-1836

Massacred as one of Fannin's men
at Goliad
Buried: Goliad.

Duty, Joseph
1801-1855

Member of Austin's Old 300
Buried: Manor Cemetery, Webberville.

Duval, Burr H.
-1836

Massacred as one of Fannin's men
at Goliad
Buried: Goliad.

Duval, John Crittenden
1816-1897

Escaped the Goliad Massacre; Was the
last survivor of Fannin's Army to die
Buried: Oakwood Cemetery, Austin.

Duvalt, Andrew
-1836

Perished defending the Alamo,
March 6, 1836, at age of 32.

Dyer, Edwin Hawley
1900-1964

Texas Sports Hall of Fame for Baseball,
Minor and Major League Coach — St.
Louis Cardinals

Buried: Garden of Gethsemane, Houston.

Dyer, George
-1836

Massacred as one of Fannin's men at Goliad
Buried: Goliad.

Dyess, William Edwin
1916-1943

World War II hero; Veteran of the Battle of Bataan, Escaped from the Death March; Reported on Japanese atrocities; Received the DSC, the Legion of Merit, Silver Star, Soldier's Medal; Dyess Air Force Base at Abilene named in his honor; Killed in plane crash in California
Buried: Albany, Texas.

Eastland, Robert Moore
-1842

Killed at the Dawson Massacre
Buried: Monument Hill, LaGrange.

Eastland, William Mosby
1806-1843

Veteran of the Battle of San Jacinto; 1st Regiment, Texas Volunteers, Company F; 1st person (and only officer) to draw a black bean (Mier Expedition)
Buried: Monument Hill, LaGrange.

Eadock, Henry H.
-1836

Killed at the Battle of Refugio in the Texas Revolution
Buried: Mt. Calvary Cemetery, Refugio.

**Eberly,
Angelina Bell Peyton**
1804?-1860

Heroine of Texas' Archives War Grave stone at Indianola washed away during a flood
Buried: Indianola.

Eddy, Andrew H.
-1836

Massacred as one of Fannin's men at Goliad
Buried: Goliad.

Edenburg, Christopher
-1846

Veteran of the Battle of San Jacinto; 2nd Regiment, Texas Volunteers, 2nd Company
Buried: near Falkey School, 18 miles N of Huntsville.

Edson, Amos B.
-1837

Veteran of the battle of San Jacinto; 1st Regiment, Regular Infantry,

Company B
Buried: City Cemetery, Houston.

Edwards, Gustavus E.
-after 1856

Member of Austin's Old 300
Buried: Wharton, Texas.

Edwards, Hayden
1771-1849

Empresario, Leader in the Fredonia
Rebellion
Buried: Nacogdoches.

Edwards, Samuel M.
-1836

Massacred as one of Fannin's men
at Goliad
Buried: Goliad.

Eels, Otis G.
-1836

Massacred as one of Fannin's men
at Goliad
Buried: Goliad.

Egbert, J. D.
-1838

Veteran of San Jacinto; 1st Regiment,
Texas Volunteers, Company B
Buried: Galveston.

Ehlinger, Joseph
1792-1845

Veteran of San Jacinto; 1st Regiment,
Texas Volunteers, Company F (William
Heard's Co.)
Buried: City Cemetery, Houston.

Ellis, James E.
-1836

Massacred as one of Fannin's men
at Goliad
Buried: Goliad.

Ellis, Michael
-1836

Massacred as one of Fannin's men
at Goliad
Buried: Goliad.

Ellis, Richard
1781-1846

Signer of the Texas Declaration of
Independence, from Virginia; Early
Settler in Texas; President of the
Convention of 1836
Buried: State Cemetery, Austin.

Ely, John
-1836

Massacred as one of Fannin's men
at Goliad
Buried: Goliad.

Emily (An Apache Girl)

See Indian Emily

English, John
1793-1868

Veteran of the Siege of Bexar and the Battle of San Jacinto
Buried: Hecks Cemetery, 10 miles E of Crockett.

English, Robert
-1836

Massacred as one of Fannin's men at Goliad
Buried: Goliad.

Erath, George Bernard
1813-1891

Veteran of San Jacinto; 1st Regiment, Texas Volunteers, Company C; With Jesse Billingsley laid out town of Waco
Buried: Oakwood Cemetery, Waco.

Escott
-1836

Massacred as one of Fannin's men at Goliad
Buried: Goliad.

Espalier, Carlos
-1836

Perished defending the Alamo, March 6, 1836, at age of 17.

Esparza, Gregorio
-1836

Perished defending the Alamo, March 6, 1836, at age of 33.

Este, Edward E.
-1843

Victim of the Mier Expedition
Buried: Monument Hill, LaGrange.

Estes, Carl Lewis
1896-1967

Publisher and industrial leader, Originator of Tyler Rose Festival
Buried: Memory Park, Longview.

Eubanks, George
-1836

Massacred as one of Fannin's men at Goliad
Buried: Goliad.

Evans, Musgrove
1810-1867

Veteran of the Battle of San Jacinto 2nd Regiment, Texas Volunteers, Company ?, Infantry
Buried: City Cemetery, LaGrange.

Evans, Robert
-1836

Perished defending the Alamo, March 6, 1836, was Master of Ordnance, age 36.

Evans, Samuel B.
-1836

Perished defending the Alamo, March 6, 1836, at age 27.

Evetts, James H.
-1856

Veteran of the Battle of San Jacinto
1st Regiment, Texas Volunteers,
Company H
Buried: Old Booneville Cemetery,
Brazos County.

Ewing,
Alexander Wray (M.D.)
1809-1853

Medical staff at San Jacinto;
Acting surgeon general; 1st Regiment,
Artillery
Buried: Episcopal Cemetery, Houston.

Ewing, James L.
-1836

Perished defending the Alamo,
March 6, 1836, at age 24.

Fadden, John
-1836

Massacred as one of Fannin's men
at Goliad
Buried: Goliad.

Fagan, John

Soldier in the Texas Revolution
Buried: Fulton.

Fannin,
James Walker (Col.)
1804-1836

Commander at Goliad (Texas Revo-
lution), Murdered by orders of Santa
Anna on March 27, 1836; Veteran of
Battles of Gonzales and Concepcion
Buried: Fannin State Park, Goliad.

Fannin, Minerva J.
1832-1893

Daughter of James W. Fannin
Buried: State Cemetery, Austin.

Fannin, Missouri Pickney
1829-1847

Daughter of James W. Fannin
Buried: Episcopal Cemetery, Galveston.

Farley, Cal
1895-1967

Veteran of World War I, Highly successful businessman; Founder of Boys'
Ranch at Old Tascosa (over 3,000 boys
cared for and educated)
Buried: Llano Cemetery, Amarillo.

Farney, Samuel
-1836

Massacred as one of Fannin's men
at Goliad
Buried: Goliad.

Farris, Lew
-1842

Killed at the Dawson Massacre
Buried: Monument Hill, LaGrange.

Farrish, Oscar
1812-1884

Veteran of the Battle of San Jacinto;
2nd Regiment, Texas Volunteers, 5th

Company, Infantry
Buried: City Cemetery, Galveston.

Fenner, Robert
-1836

Massacred as one of Fannin's men at Goliad
Buried: Goliad.

Ferguson, James Edward
1871-1944

Governor of Texas (1915-1917) Strong anti-prohibitionist, Programs included compulsory school law and liberal prison pardon policy and credit to farmers; Impeached for misapplication of public funds, removed from office.
Buried: State Cemetery, Austin.

Ferguson, Joseph G.
-1836

Massacred as one of Fannin's men at Goliad
Buried: Goliad.

Ferguson, Miriam Amanda
1875-1961

Governor of Texas (1925-1927, 1933-1935); Only female to hold highest office in state; Wife of Gov. Jim Ferguson; Administration noted for wide use of governor's parole power
Buried: State Cemetery, Austin.

Ferrell, John P.
1819-1892

Veteran of the Battle of San Jacinto; Regular Artillery Corps under James C. Neill
Buried: Thomas Cockran Cemetery, Buckhorn.

Fields, Charles
-1842

Killed at the Dawson Massacre
Buried: Monument Hill, LaGrange.

Fields, Henry
1806-1890

Veteran of the Battle of San Jacinto; 1st Regiment, Texas Volunteers, Company K
Buried: Old Magnolia Cemetery, 10 miles W of Palestine.

Fine, Charles
-1836

Massacred as one of Fannin's men at Goliad
Buried: Goliad.

Finty, Tom, Jr.
1867-1929

Accountant and lawyer, City editor of **The Galveston Tribune** (1897),

Political editor of **Tribune** and **The Dallas Morning News** (1901-1914), Editor of the **Evening Journal**, Legal counsel and editorial executive of A. H. Belo Corporation
Buried: Forest Lawn Burial Park, Dallas.

Fishbaugh, William
-1836

Perished defending the Alamo; One of 32 from Gonzales who went to the defense of the Alamo
Buried: With the heroes of the Alamo.

Fisher, John H.
-1836

Massacred as one of Fannin's men at Goliad
Buried: Goliad.

Fisher, J. K. (King)
1852-1884

Part-time outlaw, Cattle rustler; Accused of 11 murders; Assassinated with Ben Thompson in San Antonio
Buried: Uvalde.

Fisher, Samuel Rhoads
1794-1839

Signer of the Texas Declaration of Independence, from Pennsylvania, Secretary of the Texas Navy
Buried: State Cemetery, Austin.

Fisher, Rebecca Jane
1831-1926

Rescued from the Comanches, who had captured her and her brother, by Albert S. Johnston and Texas soldiers; Charter member of the Daughters of the Texas Revolution; Instrumental in aiding Clara Driscoll in saving the Alamo from being destroyed; Only woman elected to the Texas Veterans Association
Buried: Austin.

Fisher, William S.
-1845

Veteran of San Jacinto; 1st Regiment, Texas Volunteers, Company I (commander), Commander and survivor of Mier Expedition
Buried: Episcopal Cemetery, Galveston.

Fitzsimmons, Edward
-1836

Massacred as one of Fannin's men at Goliad
Buried: Goliad.

Flanders, John
-1836

Perished defending the Alamo; One of 32 from Gonzales who went to the defense of the Alamo, age of 36
Buried: With the heroes of the Alamo.

Florence, Fred Farrel
1891-1960

Dallas banker (Republic National), Civic leader, Philanthropist
Buried: Sparkman-Hillcrest, Dallas.

Flores, Manuel
1801-1868

Veteran of the Battle of San Jacinto; and the Siege of Bexar; Brother-in-law of Juan Seguin
Buried: on his ranch near Atascosa.

Floyd, Dolphin Ward
1807-1836

Perished defending the Alamo; One of 32 from Gonzales who went to the defense of the Alamo, at age of 29
Buried: With heroes of the Alamo.

Foley, Arthur G.
-1836

Massacred as one of Fannin's men at Goliad
Buried: Goliad.

Forbes, John
1797-1880

Commissary general, On Houston's staff at San Jacinto
Buried: Oak Grove Cemetery, Nacogdoches.

Ford, John Salmon (M.D.)
1815-1897

Commander of Rio Grande District during Civil War; Commander at Battle of Palmito Ranch; Congressman, Senator, Journalist, Superintendent of Texas Deaf and Dumb School
Buried: San Antonio.

Ford, Simon P.
1816-1896

Veteran of the Battle of San Jacinto; 1st Regiment, Texas Volunteers, Company A
Buried: Flatonia.

Foster, J. A.
-1836

Massacred as one of Fannin's men at Goliad
Buried: Goliad.

Forsythe, John Hubbard
-1836

Perished defending the Alamo, March 6, 1836, age of 39, Rank of Captain.

Fowle, Thomas Patton *-1836*	Killed at the Battle of San Jacinto Buried: on the field at San Jacinto.
Fowler, Andrew Jackson *1815-1885*	Veteran of the Battle of San Jacinto, 2nd Regiment, Texas Volunteers, Infantry Buried: Palestine.
Fowler, Bradford *-1836*	Massacred as one of Fannin's men at Goliad Buried: Goliad.
Fowler, Juliette Peak *1837-1889*	Established home for aged and orphans (now agency of Disciples of Christ), 1st Dallas May Queen, One of Dallas' 1st philanthropists Buried: Pioneer Memorial Park, Dallas.
Fowler, Littleton *1803-1847*	Methodist minister; Superintendent of Methodism in the Texas Republic; "Horseback" minister who established many Methodist churches in Texas Buried: Beneath altar of McMahon's Chapel, San Augustine County.
Fox, Oscar Julius *1879-1961*	Composer of western songs: **The Hills of Home; The Old Chisholm Trail; Old Paint; Whoopee Ti Yi Yo, Git Along Little Dogies**, etc. Buried: Mission Burial Park, San Antonio.
Franklin, **Benjamin Cromwell** *1805-1873*	Veteran of San Jacinto; 1st Regiment, Texas Volunteers, Company K Buried: City Cemetery N1, Galveston.
Franklin, Elijah B *-1836*	Massacred as one of Fannin's men at Goliad Buried: Goliad.
Frantz, Dalies Erhardt *1908-1965*	Eminent pianist and teacher; Concerts, Hollywood and Motion Pictures Buried: Memorial Gardens, Round Rock.

Fraser, Hugh McDonald
-1836

Massacred as one of Fannin's men at Goliad
Buried: Goliad.

Fraser, Micajah G.
-1836

Massacred as one of Fannin's men at Goliad
Buried: Goliad.

Frazer, Charles
-1836

Massacred as one of Fannin's men at Goliad
Buried: Goliad.

Frazer, William Warren
-1836

Massacred as one of Fannin's men at Goliad
Buried: Goliad.

Freeman, Thomas S.
-1836

Massacred as one of Fannin's men at Goliad
Buried: Goliad.

Friar, Daniel Boone
1800-1858

Veteran of San Jacinto;
Buried: Yorktown, Texas.

Frizzell, Terrell R.
-1836

Massacred as one of Fannin's men at Goliad
Buried: Goliad.

Frost, Hezekiah
-1836

Massacred as one of Fannin's men at Goliad
Buried: Goliad.

Fry, Benjamin Franklin
1800-1872

Veteran of Siege of Bexar and of San Jacinto; 1st Regiment, Texas Volunteers, Company I; "Fighting Parson," Baptist minister who preached under 5 flags
Buried: Jeddo Cemetery, Bastrop County.

Fuentes, Antonio
-1836

Perished defending the Alamo, March 6, 1836, at age of 23.

Fuller, Edward
-1836

Massacred as one of Fannin's men at Goliad
Buried: Goliad.

Fullinwider, Peter Hunter
1797-1867

1st Presbyterian missionary to Texas, Delivered Bibles and preached as he

traveled through East and South Texas; He, his wife and daughter died of yellow fever
Buried: Huntsville.

Fulton, George W.
1810-1893

Cattle baron; Watch and Mathematical instrument maker; Organized a company of 60 men to come from Indiana to aid in the Texas Revolution; 2nd lieutenant in regular Texas Infantry
Buried: Rockport.

Fuqua, Galva
-1836

Perished defending the Alamo; One of 32 who came from Gonzales to help defend the Alamo, at age of 16
Buried: with the heroes of the Alamo.

Furtleroy, William H.
-1836

Perished defending the Alamo, March 6, 1836, at age of 22.

Gallagher, Dominic
-1836

Massacred as one of Fannin's men at Goliad
Buried: Goliad.

Gallatin, Albert Edward
1810-1898

Veteran of the Battle of San Jacinto, 2nd Regiment, Texas Volunteers, 2nd Company
Buried: Cottonwood Cemetery, Bryan.

Gamble, David
-1836

Massacred as one of Fannin's men at Goliad
Buried: Goliad.

Gammell, William
-1869

Veteran of the Battle of San Jacinto;
Buried: Founders' Memorial Park, Houston.

Gant, William W.
1809-1840

Veteran of the Battle of San Jacinto, 1st Regiment, Texas Volunteers, Company K
Buried: Navasota.

Garey, Elijah
-1842

Killed at the Dawson Massacre
Buried: Monument Hill, LaGrange.

Garner, Edward
-1836

Massacred as one of Fannin's men at Goliad
Buried: Goliad.

Garner, John Nance
1868-1967

32nd Vice President of the United States (first Texan), Served under FDR (more conservative in his politics than FDR); Speaker of the U.S. House of Representatives; He held an important office for 38 years
Buried: Uvalde.

Garner, M. C.
-1836

Massacred as one of Fannin's men at Goliad
Buried: Goliad.

Garnet, William
-1836

Perished defending the Alamo, March 6, 1836, at age of 24.

Garrant, James W.
-1836

Perished defending the Alamo, March 6, 1836, at age of 23.

Garrett, James Girard
-1836

Perished defending the Alamo, March 6, 1836, at age of 30.

Garrison, Homer, Jr.
1901-1968

Director of Department of Public Safety and Chief of Texas Rangers; Joined the Texas Highway Patrol the year it was organized (1930)
Buried: State Cemetery, Austin.

Garvin, John E.
-1836

Perished defending the Alamo; One of 32 from Gonzales who came to the defense of the Alamo, at age of 17
Buried: with the heroes of the Alamo.

Gaston, John E.
-1836

Perished defending the Alamo; One of 32 from Gonzales who came to help defend the Alamo, at age of 17
Buried: with the heroes of the Alamo.

Gates, Amos
1799-1883

Member of Austin's Old 300
Buried: Graball Cemetery near Washington, Washington County.

Gates, Lucius W.
-1836

Massacred as one of Fannin's men at Goliad
Buried: Goliad.

Gates, William
-1829

Member of Austin's Old 300
Buried: 5 miles below Washington-on-the-Brazos.

Gathright, Thomas S.
1829-1880

1st President of Texas A&M College (now University)
Buried: Henderson.

Gatlin, William James
-1836

Massacred as one of Fannin's men at Goliad
Buried: Goliad.

Gazley,
Thomas Jefferson (M.D.)
1801-1853

Veteran of the Battle of San Jacinto, Surgeon to the Texas Army, Signer of the Texas Declaration of Independence, from New York
Buried: State Cemetery, Austin.

Gentry,
Frederick Browder
1810-1897

Veteran of the Battle of San Jacinto; 1st Regiment, Texas Volunteers, Company H
Buried: Groves-Gentry Cemetery, Hamilton.

George, James
-1836

Perished defending the Alamo; One of 32 from Gonzales who went to the defense of the Alamo, age of 34
Buried: With the heroes of the Alamo.

Germany,
Eugene Benjamin
1892-1971

Organizer and President of Lone Star Steel Co.; Writer, Politician, Mayor
Buried: Grand Saline.

Gholson, Albert G.
1818-1860

Veteran of San Jacinto, Siege of Bexar, Gonzales and Concepcion
Buried: Coryell County.

Gibbs, John
-1836

Massacred as one of Fannin's men at Goliad
Buried: Goliad.

Gibbs, Lewis C.
-1836

Killed at the Battle of Refugio in Texas Revolution
Buried: Mt. Calvary Cemetery, Refugio.

Gideon, Samuel Edward
1875-1945

Authority on early Texas architecture and culture; Aided in preserving sites;

Writer and lecturer
Buried: State Cemetery, Austin.

Giebenrath,
Imanuel Frederick
-1836

Massacred as one of Fannin's men
at Goliad
Buried: Goliad.

Gilason, Francis
-1836

Massacred as one of Fannin's men
at Goliad
Buried: Goliad.

Gilbert, William
-1836

Massacred as one of Fannin's men
at Goliad
Buried: Goliad.

Gilchrist, Gibb
1887-1972

Planner and Organizer of the Texas
A&M College system; Became its 1st
chancellor in 1948
Buried: Bryan.

Gill, John Porter
1801-1869

Veteran of the Siege of Bexar and
the Battle of San Jacinto
Buried: Ft. Bend County.

Gilland, George M.
-1836

Massacred as one of Fannin's men
at Goliad
Buried: Goliad.

Gillaspie, James
1805-1867

Veteran of the Battle of San Jacinto,
2nd Regiment, Texas Volunteers, 6th
Company, Infantry; Superintendent of
Huntsville Penitentiary
Buried: Oakwood Cemetery, Huntsville.

Gillespie, Barry
1802-1851

Assigned by Sam Houston to recruit
for the Texas Army in New Orleans
Buried: Prairie Lea Cemetery,
Brenham.

Gillespie, Robert

1st Mason buried in Texas
Buried: Richmond.

Gillett, James Buchanan
1856-1937

Texas Ranger, City Marshal of El Paso
Buried: Marfa.

Gimble, John
-1836

Massacred as one of Fannin's men
at Goliad
Buried: Goliad.

Gipson, **Frederick Benjamin** *1908-1973*	Author of **Old Yellow** (made into a popular movie,) **Savage Sam**, etc. Buried: State Cemetery, Austin.
Gladney, Edna Kahly *1905-1961*	Widely known for her work with unwed mothers; Instrumental in founding Sherman's first day nursery and Fort Worth's Texas Children's Home; Married to Sam Gladney of Gladiola Mills; Her life was played by Greer Garson in the movie "Blossoms in the Dust"; Honorary Doctor of Laws degree conferred by T.C.U. Buried: Rosehill Cemetery, Fort Worth.
Glasscock, Charles Gus *1895-1965*	Acrobat with Ringling Brothers Circus; Innovator in oil well drilling; Became offshore driller in Texas Buried: Corpus Christi.
Gleeson, John *-1836*	Massacred as one of Fannin's men at Goliad Buried: Goliad.
Gonzaullas, **Manuel TO. ("Lone Wolf")** *1893-1977*	Famous Texas Ranger Buried: Cremated at Sparkman-Hillcrest, Dallas.
Gooch, Tom Canbry *1880-1952*	Vice-president, president, general manager, editor-in-chief of the **Dallas Times Herald**; Guided the destiny of the paper and its radio station, KRLD for many years Buried: Greenwood Cemetery, Dallas.
Goodloe, Robert Kemp *1813-1879*	Veteran of the Battle of San Jacinto; Buried: Sabinetown, Sabine County.
Goodnight, Charles A. *1836-1929*	Pioneer Texas cattlemen, Blazed 3 important cattle trails; Founder of Goodnight buffalo herd; Texas Ranger during the Civil War Buried: Goodnight, Texas.
Goodrich, Benjamin Briggs *1799-1860*	Signer of the Texas Declaration of Independence, from Virginia Buried: Odd Fellows Cemetery, Anderson.

Goodrich, John Calvin
1809-1836

Perished defending the Alamo, March 6, 1836, at age of 27.

Gould,
-1836

Massacred as one of Fannin's men at Goliad
Buried: Goliad.

Grace, John C.
-1836

Massacred as one of Fannin's men at Goliad
Buried: Goliad.

Granbury, Hiram Bronson
1831-1864

Brigadier General in Confederate Army, Commander of 7th Texas of Major Gen. Pat Cleburne's Division of J. E. Johnston's (later J. Bell Hood's) Army of Tennessee; Killed at Battle of Franklin on Nov. 30, 1864
Buried: Granbury.

Graves, Ransome O.
-1836

Massacred as one of Fannin's men at Goliad
Buried: Goliad.

Gray, Francis N.
-1836

Massacred as one of Fannin's men at Goliad
Buried: Goliad.

Gray, James
1815-1884

Veteran of San Jacinto (William Warner Hill Company)
Buried: City Cemetery, Floresville.

Green, George
-1836

Massacred as one of Fannin's men at Goliad
Buried: Goliad.

Green, George
1813-1865

Veteran of the Battle of San Jacinto, 1st Regiment, Texas Volunteers, Company C
Buried: Oakhill Cemetery, Cameron.

Green, James
1805-1885

Veteran of the Battle of San Jacinto, 1st Regiment, Texas Volunteers, Company K
Buried: Burnet.

Green, Thomas J.
1814-1864

Veteran of San Jacinto, the Mier Expedition, the Somervell Expedition, and the Battle of Mansfield; Helped man the

"Twin Sisters"; Author of "Thermopylae had her messenger of defeat; the Alamo had none." Civil War General killed in service
Buried: State Cemetery, Austin.

Green, William T.
-1836

Massacred as one of Fannin's men at Goliad
Buried: Goliad.

Greer, Hilton Ross
1879-1949

Reporter, editorial writer for the **Dallas Morning News**; Author, contributor to the arts and letters of Texas
Buried: Hillcrest, Dallas.

Grieves, Davis
-1837

Veteran of San Jacinto; Regular Infantry, Company A (Henry Teal's Company)
Buried: Founders Memorial Park, Houston.

Griffin, Joe C.
-1842

Killed at the Dawson Massacre
Buried: Monument Hill, LaGrange.

Grigg, Cecil Burkett
1891-1968

Texas Sports Hall of Fame for Football, "Gray Eagle" of Rice Athletes, Backfield coach for the late Jimmy Kitts
Buried: Houston.

Grimes, Alfred Calvin
-1836

Perished defending the Alamo, March 6, 1836, at age of 23.

Grimes, James H.
-1836

Massacred as one of Fannin's men at Goliad
Buried: Goliad.

Grimes, Jesse
1788-1866

Signer of the Texas Declaration of Independence, from North Carolina
Buried: State Cemetery, Austin.

Grinolds, E. J. D.
-1836

Massacred as one of Fannin's men at Goliad
Buried: Goliad.

Groce, Jared E.
1792-1836

One of Austin's Old 300; Was the wealthiest of the group
Buried: Hempstead.

Guerrero, Jose Maria
-1836

Perished defending the Alamo, March 6, 1836, at age of 43
Buried: with the Alamo heroes.

Gunter, William
-1836

Massacred as one of Fannin's men at Goliad
Buried: Goliad.

Gwin, James C.
-1836

Perished defending the Alamo, March 6, 1836, at age of 32
Buried: with the Alamo heroes.

Hale, John C.
-1836

Killed at the Battle of San Jacinto
Buried: on the field at San Jacinto.

Hall, Harvey
-1842

Killed in the Dawson Massacre
Buried: Monument Hill, LaGrange.

Hall, John W.
1786-1845

Member of Austin's Old 300, Mason
Buried: Washington-on-the-Brazos.

Hallmark, William Calvert
1804-1880

Veteran of the Battle of San Jacinto; 2nd Regiment, Texas Volunteers, 1st Company, Infantry
Buried: Cemetery 10 miles SW of Crockett.

Hamer, Francis Augustus
1884-1955

Federal Marshal; Texas Ranger; Apprehended Clyde Barrow and Bonnie Parker at Gibsland, Louisiana, on May 23, 1934.
Buried: Austin.

Hamilton, Andrew Jackson
1815-1875

Governor of Texas (1865-66) during the Reconstruction
Buried: Oakwood Cemetery, Austin.

Hamilton, Elias E.
1816-1840

Veteran of the Battle of San Jacinto; 2nd Regiment, Texas Volunteers, 1st Company, Infantry
Buried: Oakgrove Cemetery, Nacogdoches.

Hamilton, James A.
-1836

Massacred as one of Fannin's men at Goliad
Buried: Goliad.

Hancock, George Duncan
1809-1879

Veteran of the Battle of San Jacinto (1 of 5 destroying Vince's bridge); 2nd Regiment, Texas Volunteers, 8th Company, Infantry; Veteran of Mier Expedition; Ardent Unionist
Buried: Oakwood Cemetery, Austin.

Hand, John J.
-1836

Massacred as one of Fannin's men at Goliad
Buried: Goliad.

Handy, Robert Eden
-1837

Veteran of the Battle of San Jacinto, Volunteer-aide on Houston's staff, Scout during the Texas Revolution
Buried: Richmond, Texas.

Hannum, James
-1836

Perished defending the Alamo, March 6, 1836, at age of 21
Buried: with the Alamo heroes.

Hardeman, Bailey
1795-1836

Signer of the Texas Declaration of Independence, From Tennessee
Buried: State Cemetery, Austin.

Hardeman, John Marr
1812-1857

Veteran of the Battle of San Jacinto; 1st Regiment, Texas Volunteers, Company F
Buried: Hardeman family cemetery, 1.5 miles N. of Italy, Texas.

Hardeman, William P.
1816-1898

Came to Texas in 1835 and served in every military struggle; A veteran of 4 wars; CSA General
Buried: State Cemetery, Austin.

**Hardin,
Augustine Blackburn**
1798-1891

Signer of the Texas Declaration of Independence
Buried: Hardin Family Cemetery near Liberty.

Hardin, John Gresham
1854-1937

Oilman, Philanthropist, Generous to Buckners' Orphans Home and Baptist higher institutions of learning
Buried: Burkburnett.

Hardin, John Wesley
1853-1895

"Most dangerous gunman ever in Texas"; Shot in El Paso by Constable John Selman

Buried: in Concordia Cemetery, El Paso.

Hardwick, Charles S.
-1836

Massacred as one of Fannin's men at Goliad
Buried: Goliad.

Harper,
Henry Winston (M.D.)
1859-1943

Manufacturing chemist, druggist and perfumist; Professor of Chemistry and Dean of Graduate School at U.T.
Buried: Austin.

Harper, William
-1836

Massacred as one of Fannin's men at Goliad
Buried: Goliad.

Harris, Jane Birdsall
1791-1841

Hostess of the Texas Government, March and April, 1836 Buried: Glendale Cemetery, Houston.

Harris, Jesse
-1836

Massacred as one of Fannin's men at Goliad
Buried: Goliad.

Harris, John
-1836

Perished defending the Alamo, March 6, 1836, at age of 23
Buried: with the Alamo heroes.

Harris, Robert
-1843

Victim of the Mier Expedition
Buried: Monument Hill, LaGrange.

Harris, Robert King
1912-1980

Locomotive Engineer for Texas and Pacific, Co-founder of The Dallas Archaeological Society, Publisher of the DAS Journal, Curator of SMU's Anthropology Department Collections, National Authority on artifacts of the Caddo Indian
Buried: IOOF Cemetery, Farmersville, Texas.

Harris, William
-1836

Massacred as one of Fannin's men at Goliad
Buried: Goliad.

Harrison, Andrew Jackson
-1836

Perished defending the Alamo, March 6, 1836, at age 27
Buried: with the Alamo heroes.

Harrison, Erasmus D.
-1836

Massacred as one of Fannin's men at Goliad
Buried: Goliad.

Harrison, William B.
-1836

Perished defending the Alamo, March 6, 1836, at age of 25, rank of Captain
Buried: with the Alamo heroes.

Harte, Houston
1893-1972

Newspaper man for more than 50 years, Instrumental in saving Ft. Concho and Eisenhower's birthplace in Denison
Buried: Fairmont Cemetery, San Angelo.

Harvey, John
1810-1885

Veteran of the Battle of San Jacinto, 2nd Regiment, Texas Volunteers, 1st Company, Infantry
Buried: Salado, Bell County.

Haskell, Charles M.
-1836

Perished defending the Alamo, March 6, 1836, at age of 23
Buried: with the Alamo heroes.

Haskell, Charles Ready
-1836

Massacred as one of Fannin's men at Goliad
Buried: Goliad.

Hastie, Henry
-1836

Massacred as one of Fannin's men at Goliad
Buried: Goliad.

Hatfield, William R.
-1836

Massacred as one of Fannin's men at Goliad
Buried: Goliad.

Hawkins, Joseph
-1836

Perished defending the Alamo, March 6, 1836, at age of 37
Buried: with the Alamo heroes.

Hawkins, Norborne B.
-1836

Massacred as one of Fannin's men at Goliad
Buried: Goliad.

Hawkins, William W.
1812-1886

Veteran of the Battle of San Jacinto, 1st Regiment, Texas Volunteers, Company H
Buried: Lexington, Lee County.

Hayes, E. O. ("Doc")
1906-1973

Texas Sports Hall of Fame for Basketball, Coach at S.M.U. for many years
Buried: Restland, Dallas.

Hays, John M.
-1836

Perished defending the Alamo, March 6, 1836, at age of 22
Buried: with the Alamo heroes.

Hazen, Nathaniel C.
-1836

Veteran of the Battle of San Jacinto, Led out to be shot with Fannin's men at Goliad but escaped
Buried: Presbyterian Cemetery, West Columbia.

**Heard,
William Jones Elliot**
1801-1874

Veteran of the Battle of San Jacinto; 1st Regiment, Texas Volunteers, Company F
Buried: Masonic Cemetery, Chapel Hill.

Heath, Ebenezer Smith
-1836

Massacred as one of Fannin's men at Goliad
Buried: Goliad.

Helms, Wilson
-1836

Massacred as one of Fannin's men at Goliad
Buried: Goliad.

Hemphill, William
-1836

Massacred as one of Fannin's men at Goliad
Buried: Goliad.

**Henderson, Bill
("Jitterbug")**
1919-1955

Texas Sports Hall of Fame for Basketball, Baseball, Football and Track; All-American end at A&M; State Representative (1952-1954); Died from multiple sclerosis
Buried: Forest Park Lawn, Houston.

Henderson, Bill

Texas Sports Hall of Fame for Basketball, Coach
Buried: Waco.

**Henderson,
James Pinckney**
1808-1858

Governor of Texas (1846-1847); Attorney General, Secretary of State and Foreign Minister of the Republic; Mexican War Veteran
Buried: State Cemetery, Austin.

Henderson, James Wilson
1817-1880

Governor of Texas (28 days in office 1853), Resigned to become member of U. S. Congress
Buried: Glenwood Cemetery, Houston.

Hendricks, Thomas
-1836

Perished defending the Alamo, March 6, 1836, at age of 21
Buried: with the Alamo heroes.

Henley, James
-1836

Killed at Battle of Refugio, Texas Revolution
Buried: Mt. Calvary Cemetery, Refugio.

Herndon, Patrick Henry
-1836

Perished defending the Alamo, March 6, 1836, at age of 31
Buried: with the Alamo heroes.

Herron, John H.
1815-1882

Veteran of the Battle of San Jacinto, 1st Regiment, Texas Volunteers, Company C
Buried: Family Cemetery 3 miles S of McDade.

Hersee, William
-1836

Perished defending the Alamo, March 6, 1836, at age of 32
Buried: with the Alamo heroes.

Hertzberg, Harry
-1940

Prominent San Antonio attorney, Philanthropist, Civic Leader, Concert Violinist; Left large and famed collection of Circusana to city of San Antonio
Buried: Beth-El Cemetery, San Antonio.

Heth, Joel F.
-1836

Killed at the Battle of Refugio in Texas Revolution
Buried: Mt. Calvary Cemetery, Refugio.

Heyser, John
-1836

Massacred as one of Fannin's men at Goliad
Buried: Goliad.

Hickman, John Edward
1883-1962

Texas Supreme Court Justice (1948-61)
Buried: Austin.

Hickman, Tom R. *1886-1962*	Captain in Texas Rangers, Tamed Texas oil boom towns; Traveled with Wild West Show Buried: Gainesville.
Higgins, **Michael Francis (Pinky)** *1909-1969*	Texas Sports Hall of Fame for Baseball, College and Professional Player, Coach and Scout for 39 years Buried: Hillcrest, Dallas.
Highsmith, **Benjamin Franklin** *1817-1905*	Veteran of the Siege of Bexar, the Battle of Velasco, the Battle of Gonzales and the Battle of Concepcion; Messenger from Travis and Houston to Fannin; Last man out of the Alamo and last man to bring a report from Fannin; Veteran of the Mexican War Buried: Utopia, Uvalde County.
Hill, George *-1842*	Killed in the Dawson Massacre Buried: Monument Hill, LaGrange.
Hill, Isaac Lafayette *1814-1890*	Veteran of the Battle of San Jacinto, 1st Regiment, Texas Volunteers, Company D Buried: Hill Family Cemetery, Round Top, Fayette County.
Hill, James Monroe *1818-1904*	Veteran of the Battle of San Jacinto, 1st Regiment, Texas Volunteers, Company H Buried: Oakwood Cemetery, Austin.
Hill, Robert Thomas *1858-1941*	Most distinguished professor of North American geology Cremated and ashes scattered over Round Mountain near Comanche.
Hill, Stuart *-1836*	Massacred as one of Fannin's men at Goliad Buried: Goliad.
Hitchard, John *-1836*	Massacred as one of Fannin's men at Goliad Buried: Goliad.
Hobby, William Pettus *1878-1964*	Governor of Texas (1917-1921), Youngest person ever to be governor (39

years); his program included free textbooks, Bootlegging made a felony; Editor and publisher
Buried: Glenwood Cemetery, Houston.

Hobson, Lucien
1811-1895

Veteran of the Battle of San Jacinto; 1st Regiment, Texas Volunteers, Company C
Buried: State Cemetery, Austin.

Hockaday, Ela
1875-1956

Founder of the Hockaday School for Girls in Dallas
Buried: Hillcrest, Dallas.

Hockley, George
1802-1854

On Houston's staff at San Jacinto, Inspector General; Assumed artillery command when Neill was wounded on the 20th
Buried: Bayshore Cemetery, Corpus Christi.

Hodge, Nathan
-1836

Massacred as one of Fannin's men at Goliad
Buried: Goliad.

Hogan, James
1807-1864

Veteran of the Battle of San Jacinto; Regular Infantry, Company B
Buried: City Cemetery, Houston.

Hogg, Ima
1882-1975

Outstanding philanthropist, A founder of the Houston Child Guidance Center, Instrumental in the creation of the Hogg Foundation of Mental Health at U. T., Active in the Daughters of the Republic of Texas and the Texas State Historical Association; the only daughter of Gov. James Hogg
Buried: Oakwood Cemetery, Austin.

Hogg, James Stephen
1851-1906

Governor of Texas (1891-1895), 1st native born governor; Strengthened public respect for law enforcement; "Hogg Laws" include: establishment of Railroad Commission, the Alien Land Law, restriction of amount of indebtedness by bond issues which county and municipal governments could legally undertake, Jim Crow law,

Anti-trust law
Buried: Oakwood Cemetery, Austin.

Holland, Tarpley
-1836

Perished defending the Alamo, March 6, 1836, at age of 24
Buried: with the Alamo heroes.

Holland, William H.
1849-1907

Born a slave, Educated at Oberlin College, School Teacher, State Representative; Introduced bill for establishment of Prairie View University; Instrumental in establishment of the Deaf, Dumb, and Blind Institute for Colored Youth
Buried: Mineral Wells.

House, Boyce
1896-1961

Newspaper, Writer, Poet, Well-known radio personality
Buried: Fort Worth.

House, Edward Mandell
1858-1938

Banker, Confidante of Governors and Presidents, "The Texas Warwick"; Said to have influenced U. S. policy more than any other American not holding office
Buried: Houston.

Holloway, Samuell
-1836

Perished defending the Alamo, March 6, 1836, at age of 28
Buried: with the Alamo heroes.

Homan, Harvey
-1846

Veteran of San Jacinto; 1st Regiment, Texas Volunteers, Company B
Buried: Founders Memorial Park, Houston.

Hope, James
-1836

Member of Austin's Old 300
Buried: San Felipe.

Hord, William H.
1809-1901

Founder of Oak Cliff (Hord's Ridge), 1st Dallas County Clerk, 2nd Dallas County Judge
Buried: Family Cemetery near Cedar Creek, S of Oak Cliff by the dam, Dallas.

Horn, Paul Whitfield
1870-1932

Texas Educator, 1st President of Texas Tech
Buried: Lubbock.

Hornsby, Rogers
1896-1963

Texas Sports Hall of Fame for Baseball, Greatest batsman of all time (.424 avg. in 1924 is modern record), Managed St. Louis Cardinals to 1st World Championship
Buried: Family Cemetery, Hornsby Bend few miles W of Austin.

Horseman, Headless

Unknown
Buried: Moreno Family Cemetery at La Trinidad ranch near Corpus Christi.

Horton, Alexander
1810-1894

Aide-de-camp on Houston's staff at San Jacinto
Buried: San Augustine.

Hoskins, Glenister C.
1911-1978

Marvelous Philosopher and Professor of Education at S.M.U.; In his long bout with cancer (18 years) he lived what he taught
Buried: Restland, Dallas.

Houston, Andrew Jackson
1854-1941

U. S. Senator from Texas (oldest to serve at age of nearly 87; served only 24 days), Son of Sam Houston
Buried: On the San Jacinto Battlefield.

Houston, Margaret Bell
1877-1966

Poet, Novelist, Short story writer, Granddaughter of Sam Houston
Buried: Restland, Dallas.

Houston, Margaret Lea
1819-1867

Wife of Sam Houston
Buried: City Cemetery, Independence.

Houston, Margaret Lea
  (Mrs. Weston Williams)
1848-1906

Daughter of Sam Houston
Buried: Glenwood Cemetery, Houston.

Houston, Mary Willie
1850-1931

Daughter of Margaret and Sam Houston
Buried: Abilene, Texas.

Houston, Nancy Elizabeth
(Mrs. Joseph Morrow)
1846-1920

Daughter of Sam Houston
Buried: Glenwood Cemetery, Houston.

Houston, Samuel
1793-1863

Governor of Tennessee and of Texas (1859-1861), President of the Republic of Texas, U. S. Congressman from

Tennessee, U. S. Senator from Texas, Self-educated, Adopted son of a Cherokee Chief, School teacher, Participant in Battle of Horseshoe Bend with Andrew Jackson, General of Texas Revolutionary Armies (1835-1836); Opposed to secession, Deposed from office of Governor as he declined to take the oath of allegiance to the Confederate Government
Buried: Huntsville.

Houston, Sam, Jr.
1843-1894

Confederate soldier, Taken prisoner at Battle of Shiloh; Studied medicine at University of Pennsylvania, Author of articles and short stories
Buried: City Cemetery, Independence.

Houston, William Rogers
1858-1920

Son of Margaret and Sam Houston
Buried: Oak Cliff Cemetery, Dallas.

Howell, William D.
-1836

Perished defending the Alamo, March 6, 1836, at age of 45; Surgeon
Buried: with the Alamo heroes.

Howth, William Edward
1810-1859

Veteran of the Siege of Bexar
Buried: Masonic Cemetery, Chapel Hill.

**Hubbard,
Richard Bennett**
1832-1901

Governor of Texas (1876-1879), Ridded the state of much lawlessness: Sam Bass, Bill Longley, John Wesley Hardin, King Fisher and Ben Thompson met their end while he was governor. Great orator, Cavalry commander in the Confederate Army
Buried: Oakwood Cemetery, Tyler.

Hufty, Edward
-1836

Massacred as one of Fannin's men at Goliad
Buried: Goliad.

Hughes, Howard
1906-1976

Millionaire recluse, Aircraft designer, Test pilot, Flew around the world in 3 days in 1938; Co-founder of Hughes Tool Co., Movie Maker
Buried: Houston.

Hughes, John Reynolds
1855-1947

Friend of the Indians, Quanah Parker in particular Texas Ranger (1887-1915,) longest service in Ranger history
Buried: State Cemetery, Austin.

Hughes, Wesley
-1836

Massacred as one of Fannin's men at Goliad
Buried: Goliad.

Hughes, Wiley
-1836

Massacred as one of Fannin's men at Goliad
Buried: Goliad.

Hulen, John Augustus
1871-1957

Veteran of the Spanish American War and World War I, Many awards for gallantry, Commander of the 36th Army Division after WWI, Adjutant General of Texas
Buried: Palacios.

Humphries, Jesse C.
-1836

Killed at the Battle of Refugio in the Texas Revolution
Buried: Mt. Calvary Cemetery, Refugio.

Hunt, Haroldson Lafayette
1889-1974

Texas billionaire, Oilman, Called the "World's Greatest Wildcatter"
Buried: Hillcrest Cemetery, Dallas.

Hunt, John Campbell
1811-1840

Veteran of the Battle of San Jacinto; 1st Regiment, Texas Volunteers, Company H
Buried: Cemetery near Smithville.

Hunt, Francis M.
-1836

Massacred as one of Fannin's men at Goliad
Buried: Goliad.

Hunt, Joel
1905-1978

Texas Sports Hall of Fame for Football
Buried: Teague

**Hunter,
Johnson Calhoun (M.D.)**
1787-1855

Member of Austin's Old 300
Buried: Brick Church Graveyard between San Felipe and Liberty.

Hunter, William
-1836

Massacred as one of Fannin's men at Goliad
Buried: Goliad.

Hurst, Stephen Decatur
-1836

Massacred as one of Fannin's men at Goliad.
Buried: Goliad.

Hyer, Robert Stewart
1860-1929

Physicists and University President, Designed 1st wireless station in Texas (1904); Pioneered X-Ray in the Southwest
Buried: Crown Hill Cemetery, Dallas.

Hyland, Joseph
1804-1898

Veteran of the Battle of San Jacinto, 1st Regiment, Texas Volunteers, Company F
Buried: Bagdad Cemetery near Leander, Williamson County.

Indian Emily
-1879

Killed by accident while warning Fort Davis of an Indian attack
Buried: Fort Davis.

Inglish, Bailey
1793-1867

Built Fort Inglish on outskirts of present day Bonham; Served as postmaster and land commissioner
Buried: 1 block S of fort, Bonham.

Ingram, Ira
1788-1837

Member of Austin's Old 300
Buried: Matagorda.

Ingram, John
1808-1896

Veteran of San Jacinto; 1st Regiment Texas Volunteers, Company H
Buried: Fairmont Cemetery, San Angelo.

Ingram, Seth
1790-1857

Member of Austin's Old 300
Buried: Matagorda.

Ireland, John
1836-1896

Governor of Texas (1883-1887), Alamo purchased, fence cutting made a felony
Buried: State Cemetery, Austin.

Irion,
Robert Anderson (M.D.)
1806-1861

Secretary of State under Houston
Buried: Oakgrove Cemetery, Nacogdoches.

Irvine, Josephus Somerville
1819-1876

Veteran of Siege of Bexar and San Jacinto; 2nd Regiment under Sidney Sherman and Capt. Benjamin F. Bryant

Irvine, Robert Boyd
1813-1836

Buried: Wilson's Chapel, Newton County.

Veteran of Concepcion, Assistant Quartermaster, Brother of Josephus
Buried: San Augustine.

Isbell, James H.
1814-1858

Veteran of San Jacinto; 1st Regiment, Texas Volunteers, Company D
Buried: South Belton Cemetery, Belton.

Jack, James C.
-1836

Massacred as one of Fannin's men at Goliad
Buried: Goliad.

Jack, Patrick Churchill
1808-1844

Revolutionary figure, Imprisoned with Travis at Anahuac
Buried: State Cemetery, Austin.

Jack, William Houston
1806-1844

Veteran of the Battle of San Jacinto, 2nd Regiment, Texas Volunteers, 4th Company, Infantry
Buried: Lakeview Cemetery, Galveston.

Jackson, John N.
-1836

Massacred as one of Fannin's men at Goliad
Buried: Goliad.

Jackson, Thomas
-1836

Perished defending the Alamo; One of 32 who went from Gonzales to help defend the Alamo
Buried: With the heroes of the Alamo.

Jackson, William Daniel
-1836

Perished defending the Alamo, March 6, 1836, at age of 29
Buried: with the Alamo heroes.

James, John
-1836

Massacred as one of Fannin's men at Goliad
Buried: Goliad.

Jameson, Green, B.
1807-1836

Perished defending the Alamo; Aide and chief engineer, with rank of ensign for the Texas forces at the Alamo.
Buried: with the Alamo heroes.

Jaques, Isaac L.
-1836

Veteran of San Jacinto; 2nd Regiment, Texas Volunteers, 5th Company,

Infantry
Buried: San Jacinto State Park.

Jefferson, Blind Lemon
1897?-1929

Black composer of blues music,
Recognized as one of the earliest
representatives of the "classic blues"
field
Buried: Wortham Negro Cemetery,
Wortham.

Jennings, Charles B.
-1836

Massacred as one of Fannin's men
at Goliad
Buried: Goliad.

Jennings, Gordon C.
-1836

Perished defending the Alamo,
March 6, 1836, at age of 27
Buried: with the Alamo heroes.

Jester, Beauford Halbert
1893-1949

Governor of Texas (1947-1949),
Gilmer-Aiken laws and Right to Work
law during his term; 1st governor to die
in office
Buried: Corsicana.

Jett, James Mathew
-1845

Veteran of San Jacinto; 1st Regiment,
Texas Volunteers, Company B
Buried: Galveston.

Johnson, "Arkansas"

Desperado, Partner of Sam Bass
Buried: Salt Creek near Springton.

Johnson, David
-1836

Massacred as one of Fannin's men
at Goliad
Buried: Goliad.

Johnson, Edward J.
-1836

Massacred as one of Fannin's men
at Goliad
Buried: Goliad.

Johnson, Francis White
1799-1884

Representatives to the Convention of
1832. Texas Army Volunteer, Veteran
of the Siege of Bexar, Led 1 of 2 units on
the ill-fated Matamoros Expedition; In
command at taking of the Alamo in 1835
Buried: State Cemetery, Austin.

Johnson, Lewis
-1836

Perished defending the Alamo, March 6, 1836
Buried: with the Alamo heroes.

Johnson, Lyndon Baines
1908-1973

36th President of the United States; U. S. Congressman and Senator, (won Senate seat over Coke Stevenson by infamous 87 votes), Backed FDR almost 100%, Fought against Senator Joseph McCarthy, Became Senate Majority leader in 1955; Vice-President under John F. Kennedy, Assumed presidency when Kennedy was assassinated, Elected to second term; His program was the "Great Society", Much civil rights legislation passed; Country dissatisfied and belligerent over escalation of war in Viet Nam
Buried: LBJ Ranch at Stonewall.

Johnson,
John Drew ("Boody")
1905-1967

Texas Sports Hall of Fame for Football
Buried: Waco.

Johnson, William
-1836

Perished defending the Alamo, March 6, 1836
Buried: with the Alamo heroes.

Johnson, William R.
-1836

Killed at the Battle of Refugio in the Texas Revolution
Buried: Mt. Calvary Cemetery, Refugio.

Johnston, Albert Sidney
1803-1862

West Point graduate, Veteran of the Black Hawk War, Secretary of State for U. S., Veteran of Mexican War, General, Western Department, Confederate Army, Won the Battle of Shiloh but was killed in the action there; One of the great military minds of the Confederacy
Buried: State Cemetery, Austin.

Johnston, Siddie Jo
1905-1976

Author of books for children, Librarian of the children's section of Dallas Public Library for many years
Buried: Corpus Christi.

Johnston, William P.
-1836

Massacred as one of Fannin's men at Goliad
Buried: Goliad.

Joiner,
Columbus Marvin (Dad)
1860-1947

Drilled the oil well, the Daisy Bradford N3, in September of 1930; became the father of the great East Texas Oil Field
Buried: Hillcrest Mausoleum, Dallas.

Jones, Anson (M.D.)
1798-1858

Last President of the Republic of Texas; Surgeon on Medical staff at San Jacinto, 2nd Regiment, Texas Volunteers; Established 1st Masonic Lodge in Texas (1835-Holland Lodge N36 at Brazoria)
Buried: Glenwood Cemetery, Houston.

Jones, Asa
-1842

Killed at the Dawson Massacre
Buried: Monument Hill, LaGrange.

Jones, Henry W.
-1836

Massacred as one of Fannin's men at Goliad
Buried: Goliad.

Jones, James W.
1797-1847

Member of Austin's Old 300; With his brother, found Mrs. Jane Long on the San Jacinto River and took her to San Antonio
Buried: private cemetery, Prairie Lea.

Jones, Jesse Holman
1874-1956

Lumberman, banker and statesman; Held many positions in the Federal government; Conservative Democrat; "Mr. Houston"; Philanthropist and civic leader
Buried: Forest Park Cemetery, Houston.

Jones, John
-1842

Killed in the Dawson Massacre
Buried: Monument Hill, LaGrange.

Jones, John
-1836

Perished defending the Alamo, March 6, 1836, at age of 26
Buried: with the Alamo heroes.

Jones, John B.
-1881

Texas Ranger, Frontier force commander, Adjutant general of Texas, Trapped the outlaw Sam Bass
Buried: Oakwood Cemetery, Austin.

Jones,
Margaret Virginia (Margo)
1913-1955

Instructor of drama, Director of Broadway plays, Creator of the "Theater in the Round" in the U. S., Producer of 85 plays
Buried: Livingston, Texas.

Jones, Oliver
1794-1866

Member of Austin's Old 300; Designed present day state flag
Buried: State Cemetery, Austin.

Jones, Preston
1936-1979

1st and foremost of Texas playwrights, Author of **Texas Trilogy** and **The Last Meeting of the Knights of the White Magnolia**
Buried: Hillcrest, Dallas.

Jones, Randall
1786-1873

Member of Austin's Old 300
Buried: Houston.

Jones, Thomas L.
-1842

Victim of the Mier Expedition
Buried: Monument Hill, LaGrange.

Jordan, Louis John
1890-1918

1st Texas officer to lose his life in World War I, First Southern man to be named on an All-American football team (Texas Longhorns)
Buried: City Cemetery, Fredericksburg.

Jordan, Thomas J.
1816-1884

Soldier in the Texas Army (1836)
Buried: Milford Cemetery, Milford, Texas.

Joske, Alexander
1866-1926

Founder of Joske's Department Stores (first one in San Antonio, "The Largest Store in the Largest State")
Buried: Temple Beth-El Mausoleum, San Antonio.

Justin,
Herman Joseph (Joe)
1859-1918

Pioneer Texas Bootmaker
Buried: Nocona Cemetery, Nocona.

Kahn, Emanual Meyer
-1923

Founder of the E. M. Kahn Clothing Stores in Dallas (1872), One of the founders of Temple Emanuel in Dallas
Buried: Emanuel Cemetery, Dallas.

Kalita	Chief of the Alabama and Coushatta Indian Tribes during the Texas Revolution, Scout for Sam Houston Buried: Moss Hill 15 miles N of Liberty.
Karner, John *1816-1901*	Company A, Regular Infantry at the the Battle of San Jacinto Buried: Mexia.
Karnes, Henry Wax *1812-1840*	Veteran of the Battle of San Jacinto; 2nd Regiment, Texas Volunteers, Calvary Scout Buried: San Antonio.
Kaufman, David *1813-1851*	1st U. S. Congressman from Texas, Charter member of the Philosophical Society of Texas, Kaufman County named for him Buried: State Cemetery, Austin.
Kell, Frank *1859-1941*	One of the leading builders of Wichita Falls; Miller, oil and cattleman, Railroad construction; Philanthropist Buried: Riverside Cemetery, Wichita Falls.
Kelly, George Addison *1832-1909*	Early manufacturer of cow bells, Founder of Kelly Plow Company in Longview (the only full line plow company in the Southwest) Buried: Greenwood Cemetery, Longview.
Kelly, James *-1836*	Massacred as one of Fannin's men at Goliad Buried: Goliad.
Kelly, John *-1836*	Massacred as one of Fannin's men at Goliad Buried: Goliad.
Kellogg, Johnny *-1836*	Perished defending the Alamo; One of 32 who went from Gonzales to help defend the Alamo, at age of 19 Buried: with the heroes of the Alamo.
Kelso, Alfred *1808-1895*	Veteran of the Battle of San Jacinto; 1st Regiment, Texas Volunteers,

	Company F Buried: Brite Cemetery, Atascosa County.
Kemp, James P. *-1836*	Massacred as one of Fannin's men at Goliad Buried: Goliad.
Kemp, Louis Wiltz *1881-1956*	Executive with Texas Co. (Texaco), One of the best informed men on Texas History, Major force in rejuvenating care of the state cemetery Buried: State Cemetery, Austin.
Kenedy, Mifflin *1818-1895*	Partner with Richard King in the King Ranch (1860-1868), Among first ranchers in Texas to use fence (smooth wire); Railroad construction Buried: Brownsville.
Kenney, James *-1836*	Perished defending the Alamo, March 6, 1836, at age of 22 Buried: with the Alamo heroes.
Kent, Andrew *-1836*	Perished defending the Alamo; One of 32 from Gonzales who went to the defense of the Alamo, at age of 38 Buried: with the heroes of the Alamo.
Kerr, Joseph *-1836*	Perished defending the Alamo, March 6, 1836, at age of 22 Buried: with the Alamo heroes.
Kiest, Edwin John *1861-1942*	Owner and publisher of the **Dallas Times Herald,** Philanthropist Buried: Oakland Cemetery, Dallas.
Kimball, Justin Ford *1872-1956*	Teacher, lawyer, superintendent of Dallas Independent School District, Organizer of Blue Cross Hospitalization Plan (first hospital insurance plan in the nation) Buried: Sparkman-Hillcrest, Dallas.
Kimbell, Kay *1861-1964*	President of Kimbell Milling Company, Established the Kimbell Art Foundation in Fort Worth in 1936

(present day Kimbell Art Museum)
Buried: Whitewright.

Kimble, George C.
-1836

Perished defending the Alamo; One of 32 from Gonzales who went to the defense of the Alamo at age of 26
Buried: with the heroes of the Alamo.

Kimbro, William
-1836

Veteran of the Battle of San Jacinto; 2nd Regiment, Texas Volunteers, 8th Company, Infantry
Buried: Old Cemetery, Palestine.

King, Amon Butler
1807-1836

Captain of the Paducah Volunteers. Ordered to extricate stranded families from Refugio, Ambushed by Mexican "Rancheros"; Took refuge in the mission of Nuestra Senora del Refugio, Sent to Fannin for help. Col. William Ward came to relief. King refused to return to Goliad until he had punished the rancheros. His insubordination was probably cause of Fannin's ultimate disaster. King and his party were shot by the rancheros
Buried: Mt. Calvary Cemetery, Refugio.

King, John G.
-1836

Perished defending the Alamo; One of 32 from Gonzales who went to the defense of the Alamo at age of 26
Buried: with the heroes of the Alamo.

King, Montgomery B.
-1836

Massacred as one of Fannin's men at Goliad
Buried: Goliad.

King, Richard
1824-1885

Founder of the King Ranch and developer of the Santa Gertrudis breed
Buried: Kingsville.

King, Samuel Alexander
1834-1923

Presbyterian minister, Served 1st Church in Waco for 40 years; Teacher and member of directing board of Austin Seminary
Buried: Oakwood Cemetery, Waco.

King, William P.
-1836

Perished defending the Alamo; One of 32 who went from Gonzales to help

defend the Alamo, at age of 24
Buried: With the heroes of the Alamo.

Kinney, Allen O.
-1836

Massacred as one of Fannin's men at Goliad
Buried: Goliad.

Kirk, Harvey
-1836

Killed at the Battle of Refugio in the Texas Revolution
Buried: Mt. Calvary Cemetery, Refugio.

Kirkland, Olea Forest
1892-1949

Indian Rock art painter and collector, Founder of the Dallas Archaeological Society
Buried: Laurel Land Cemetery, Dallas.

Kirkley, Bertha
1868-1949

Texas History teacher at Sam Houston State Teacher College, Began successful movement to purchase the Huntsville home of Sam Houston and its perpetuation as a historic shrine
Buried: Oakwood, Cemetery, Huntsville.

Kissam, P. T.
-1836

Massacred as one of Fannin's men at Goliad
Buried: Goliad.

Kitts, Jimmy
1921-1975

Texas Sports Hall of Fame for Basketball
Buried: Dallas.

Kleberg, Richard Mifflin
1887-1955

Foreman and part owner of the King Ranch (1913-1924), Son of Alice Gertrudis King Kleberg and Robert Kleberg; Staunch Democrat, Served in Congress for 5 terms, Friend of Lyndon B. Johnson, Backed Dewey over FDR
Buried: Chamberlain Memorial Park, Kingsville.

Kleberg, Robert Justus
1803-1888

Veteran of the Battle of San Jacinto, 1st Regiment, Texas Volunteers, Company D
Buried: family cemetery on ranch near Yorktown, Texas.

Kleberg, Robert Justus
1853-1932

Son of Robert J. Kleberg (above) Assumed control of King Ranch after

Richard King's death; Married King's daughter, Excellent ranch manager
Buried: family cemetery on ranch near Yorktown, Texas.

Knight, James
1787-1858

Member of Austin's Old 300
Buried: Kirk's Point, Fort Bend County.

Knight, Obadiah
1808-1868

Donated 1st land in Dallas area for the purpose of a school
Buried: Cochran Chapel Cemetery, Dallas.

Knott, John Francis
1878-1963

Political cartoonist with the **Dallas Morning News**, Creator of "Old Man Texas", Pulitzer Prize citation in 1936, Greatly interested in art education and taught many years in the Dallas Public Evening School
Buried: Restland Cemetery, Dallas.

Koch, Botchey
1906-1964

Texas Sports Hall of Fame for Football
Buried: Temple, Texas.

Kornegay, David Smith
1810-1856

Veteran of the Battle of San Jacinto: 1st Regiment, Texas Volunteers, Company H
Buried: Cemetery 1 mile N of Bosqueville, McLennan County.

Kornicky, John
-1836

Massacred as one of Fannin's men at Goliad
Buried: Goliad.

Kraatz, Lewis
-1857

Veteran of the Battle of San Jacinto; 2nd Regiment, Texas Volunteers, Infantry
Buried: Independence, Washington County.

Kraft, Clarence
1887-1958

Texas Sports Hall of Fame for Baseball
Buried: Fort Worth.

Krebs, James Rowland
1935-1965

Texas Sports Hall of Fame for Basketball
Buried: Restland, Dallas.

Kurth, Ernest Lynn
1885-1960

Industrialist and philanthropist,
Owner of Southland Paper Mills
Buried: Glendale Cemetery, Lufkin.

Kuykendall, Abner
-1834

Member of Austin's Old 300
Buried: 4 miles S of Independence.

Kuykendall, Barzillai
-after 1846

Member of Austin's Old 300, Son of
Abner Kuykendall
Buried: 4 miles S of Independence.

Kuykendall, Joseph
-1878

Member of Austin's Old 300, Brother
of Abner Kuykendall
Buried: 4 miles S of Independence.

Labadie,
Nicholas Descomps (M.D.)
1801-1867

Veteran of the Battle of San Jacinto,
1st Regiment, Texas Volunteers,
Medical Staff
Buried: Catholic Cemetery, Galveston.

Lamar,
Mirabeau Bounaparte
1798-1859

President of the Republic of Texas
(1838-1841); Father of public education
in Texas; Veteran of the Battle of San
Jacinto, 2nd Regiment, Texas
Volunteers, Cavalry Commander;
Secretary of War; Commander of Texas
Army after San Jacinto; Favored
expansion of Texas to the Pacific (Santa
Fe Expedition); Anti-Indian
Buried: Morton Cemetery, Richmonnd,
Texas.

Lamb, George A.
1814-1836

Killed at the Battle of San Jacinto
Buried: On the field at San Jacinto.

Lambert, Walter
1808-1865

Veteran of the Battle of San Jacinto,
1st Regiment, Texas Volunteers,
Company K; Texas Ranger; Civil
Servant
Buried: Cemetery in Copano, Refugio
County.

Lamond, Adams G.
-1836

Massacred as one of Fannin's men
at Goliad
Buried: Goliad.

Lyndon Baines Johnson

Margaret Lea Houston and Nancy Lea

Collin Aldrich

Nelson Box

George W. Littlefield

John Andrew Box

Monument, LaGrange — Dawson Men Killed at Salado

Thomas Griffin Box

Pompeo Coppini

Albert Sidney Johnston

Stephen F. Austin

Rogers Hornsby

Helena Dill Berryman   Maureen Connolly Brinker

Adolph Toepperwein

Eugene C. Barker

Edward Burleson

Haroldson Lafayette Hunt

Kearle Lee Berry

James Frank Dobie

Walter Prescott Webb

Harry Arthur McArdle

Hugh McLeod

Oscar Julius Fox

Samuel Taliaferro Rayburn

Edgar Tobin

Robert Cooke Buckner

William Ware

Oscar Branch Colquitt

Beaumont Bonaparte Buck

Everett Lee DeGolyer

Robert McAlpin Williamson

John Austin Wharton

Ashbel Smith

Anna Pennybacker

Ima Hogg

Louis Wiltz Kemp

Suzanna Dickinson (Hannig)

Monument at LaGrange — Black Bean Victims

Grave Monument at Goliad, Fannin and Men

Candace Midkiff Bean

Robert Emmet Bledsoe Baylor

"THE WORLD WILL
TAKE CARE OF
HOUSTON'S FAME"
"ANDREW JACKSON"

Sam Houston

Lancaster, Joseph
1816-1874

Veteran of the Battle of San Jacinto,
Early journalist in Texas
Buried: Austin.

Landrum, Lynn Wiley
1891-1961

Editorial writer for the **Dallas Morning News**, His column "Thinking Out Loud" read and enjoyed by many people
Buried: Whitewright, Texas.

Lane, Walter Payne
1817-1892

Veteran of the Battle of San Jacinto; 2nd Regiment, Texas Volunteers, Cavalry; Brought back to Texas the remains of the Mier Expedition men in 1843; Served as Brigadier General in Confederate Army
Buried: Marshall, Texas.

Lang, George Washington
-1883

Veteran of the Battle of San Jacinto; Company A, Regular Infantry
Buried: San Saba.

Lanham, Samuel Willis
1846-1908

Governor of Texas (1903-1907), State banks established, Terrell election law passed; Last Confederate veteran to serve as governor
Buried: Greenwood Cemetery, Weatherford, Texas.

Lantz, Charles
-1836

Massacred as one of Fannin's men at Goliad
Buried: Goliad.

La Salle, Rene Robert Cavalier Sieur de
1643-1687

French explorer, in 1685 led expedition which led to French claims to Texas
Buried: near Navasota (?).

Latimer, Albert Hamilton
1808-1877

Signer of the Texas Declaration of Independence from Tennessee
Buried: Clarksville.

Law, Robert Adger
1879-1961

Well-known professor of English, Taught at U. T. in Austin for 51 years
Buried: Oakwood Cemetery, Austin.

Lawrence, Joseph
-1896

Veteran of the Battle of San Jacinto, 2nd Regiment, Texas Volunteers, Cavalry

Buried: Hackberry Cemetery, Navarro County.

Lea, Edmond

2nd in command of the Union warship, the **Harriet Lane** during the Battle of Galveston; Wounded, and died in his Confederate father's arms (father had boarded ship)
Buried: Episcopal Cemetery, Galveston.

Lea, Nancy Moffette
1780-1864

One of the organizers of the Baptist Church in Texas; Mother of Margaret Lea Houston (wife of Sam Houston)
Buried: Independence.

League, Hosea H.
-1837

Member of Austin's Old 300
Buried: Harrisburg.

Ledbetter, Snead
-1836

Killed at the Battle of Refugio in the Texas Revolution
Buried: Mt. Calvary Cemetery, Refugio.

Lee, Green
-1836

Massacred as one of Fannin's men at Goliad
Buried: Goliad.

Lee, Harper Baylor
1884-1941

Famous matador, Probably the greatest non-Latin bull fighter.
Buried: San Antonio.

Lee, Umphrey
1893-1958

Prominent Methodist minister and educator, President of S.M.U. (1939-1954)
Buried: Restland, Dallas.

Lefevre, Arthur
1863-1928

Texas educator
Buried: Houston.

Legrand, Edwin Oswald
1803-1871

Signer of the Texas Declaration of Independence, from North Carolina; Veteran of the Battle of San Jacinto and the Siege of Bexar; 2nd Regiment, Texas Volunteers, 8th Company, Infantry
Buried: 10 miles S of Graham Cemetery, San Augustine.

Leslie, John Douglass
1860-1935

Very prominent early Presbyterian leader
Buried: Oakland Cemetery, Dallas.

Lester, James S.
1799-1879

Veteran of the Battle of San Jacinto, 1st Regiment, Texas Volunteers, Company F
Buried: City Cemetery, LaGrange.

LeTourneau, Robert Gilmore
1888-1969

Contractor and builder of land leveling equipment and off-shore oil rigs, Philanthropist
Buried: Longview.

Leverett, Oscar B.
-1836

Massacred as one of Fannin's men at Goliad
Buried: Goliad.

Lewis, Archibald S.
-1839

Veteran of the Battle of San Jacinto; 2nd Regiment, Texas Volunteers, 7th Company (Benjamin F. Bryant's Company)
Buried: Founders' Memorial Park, Houston.

Lewis, John E.
1808-1883

Veteran of the Battle of San Jacinto, 1st Regiment, Texas Volunteers, Company F
Buried: City Cemetery, LaGrange.

Lewis, Nathaniel C.
1806-1872

Last Anglo to leave the Alamo before the massacre; Not held in contempt
Buried: San Antonio.

Lewis, Patrick
-1836

Killed at the Dawson Massacre
Buried: Monument Hill, LaGrange.

Lewis, William Irvin
-1836

Perished defending the Alamo, March 6, 1836, at age of 23.

Lightfoot, William J.
-1836

Perished defending the Alamo, March 6, 1836, at age of 25, rank of 3rd corporal
Buried: with the Alamo heroes.

Lincecum, Gideon D.
1793-1873

Internationally famous botanist and naturalist, Friend of Darwin
Buried: State Cemetery, Austin.

Lindheimer,
Ferdinand Joseph
1801-1879

"Father of Texas Botany," Editor
Buried: New Braunfels.

Lindley, Johathan L.
-1836

Perished defending the Alamo, March 6, 1836, at age of 31; One of 32 from Gonzales who went to help defend the Alamo
Buried: with the heroes of the Alamo.

Linvely, Charles
-1836

Massacred as one of Fannin's men at Goliad
Buried: Goliad.

Linn, John Joseph
1798-1885

Last alcalde and 1st mayor of Victoria, Veteran of the Battle of Gonzales, Texas Army Quartermaster
Buried: Evergreen Cemetery, Victoria.

Linn, William
-1836

Perished defending the Alamo, March 6, 1836.

Linn, William
-1842

Killed at the Dawson Massacre
Buried: Monument Hill, LaGrange.

Lipscomb,
Kleber VanZandt
1884-1979

Co-owner and operator of Tennessee Dairies, Inc. (later Foremost Food Co.); Helped organize Jarvis Christian College; Board member and president of Juliet Fowler Home for Orphans and Aged; Board member of National Benevolent Association
Buried: Sparkman-Hillcrest, Dallas.

Littlefield,
George Washington
1842-1920

Cattleman and banker; Major in Confederate Army (19 years old), Terry's Texas Rangers; Furnished money for U. T. library to buy books on the South
Buried: Oakwood Cemetery, Austin.

Litton, John
1812-1856

Soldier of the San Jacinto army
Buried: State Cemetery, Austin.

Logan, John C.
-1836

Massacred as one of Fannin's men at Goliad
Buried: Goliad

Logan, William M.
1810-1836

Veteran of San Jacinto 2nd Regiment, Texas Volunteers, 3rd Company, Infantry; was marching to the Alamo when learned of its fall
Buried: Presbyterian Cemetery, West Columbia.

Lomax, John Avery
1867-1948

Folklorist, Collector/composer of cowboy ballads and folk songs
Buried: Oakwood Cemetery, Austin.

Long,
Jane Herbert Wilkinson
1798-1880

"The Mother of Texas," Member Austin's Old 300; Bore the first known white child in Texas (Dec. 21, 1821, her 3rd child); Survived the winter of 1821 at Bolivar Point, Rescued by Randal and James W. Jones in 1822
Buried: Morton Cemetery, Richmond.

Long, John Lawson
1859-1933

Educator, Superintendent of the Dallas Schools (1893-1908), Manager of Southern Printing Company (1908-1914), President of Practical Drawing Co. (1916-1933), Member of the board of trustees of George Peabody College
Buried: Restland Cemetery, Dallas.

Longley, William Preston
1851-1878

Outlaw, Committed 32 murders, Hanged
Buried: Giddings Cemetery, Giddings.

Losoyo, Toribio Domingo
-1836

Perished defending the Alamo, March 6, 1836
Buried: with the Alamo heroes.

Lott, Uriah
1842-1915

Early railroad developer
Buried: Kingsville.

Loverly, Alexander J.
-1836

Massacred as one of Fannin's men at Goliad
Buried: Goliad.

Loving, James C.
1836-1902

Cattleman, One of the founders of the Cattle Raisers Association, Son of Oliver Loving
Buried: Weatherford.

Loving, Joseph
-1836

Massacred as one of Fannin's men at Goliad
Buried: Goliad.

Loving, Oliver
1812-1867

"Dean of the Texas Trail Drivers," Goodnight-Loving trail from Texas; Killed by Comanches
Buried: Greenwood Cemetery, Weatherford.

Lubbock, Francis Richard
1815-1905

Governor of Texas during the Civil War (1861-1863), Helped to organize the Democratic Party in Texas
Buried: State Cemetery, Austin.

Luders, Henry
-1836

Veteran of the Battle of San Jacinto, Company B, Regular Infantry
Buried: Galveston.

Lynch, A. M.
-1836

Massacred as one of Fannin's men at Goliad
Buried: Goliad.

Lynch, Nathanael

Member of Austin's Old 300
Buried: Lynchburg.

Lynch, Nicholas
-1851

Veteran of the Battle of San Jacinto; Regular Infantry
Buried: Liberty County.

Lynde, A. H.
-1836

Massacred as one of Fannin's men at Goliad
Buried: Goliad.

Magill, William Harrison
1813-1878

Veteran of the Battle of San Jacinto, 1st Regiment, Texas Volunteers, Company C
Buried: Burnet, Texas

Magruder, John Bankhead
1810-1871

General in the Confederate Army, Won the Battle of Galveston, Later joined Maximillian's Army as a major general
Buried: Galveston.

Mahan, Patrick
-1843

Veteran of the Mier Expedition, Drew a black bean and was executed
Buried: Monument Hill, LaGrange.

Mahoney, Dennis
-1836

Massacred as one of Fannin's men at Goliad
Buried: Goliad.

Main, George Washington
-1836

Perished defending the Alamo, March 6, 1836, at age of 29
Buried: with the Alamo heroes.

Malone, William T.
1817-1836

Died with the Alamo defenders, at age of 18; Name does not appear on the rolls, but his presence was vouched for by Joe (Travis' servant), Benjamin Highsmith and Mrs. Almaron Dickinson.

Mansbendel, Peter H.
1883-1940

Swiss woodcarver, Portrayed Texas themes as historic people, places and events (1915-1940)
Buried: Oakwood Cemetery, Auston.

Marks, Tom M.

Founder of the 4-H Clubs — called the first one the "Boys' Corn Club"
Buried: Jacksboro.

Marquis, Robert Lincoln
1880-1934

Texas educator
Buried: Denton.

Marsh, Shubael
-1865

Member of Austin's Old 300
Buried: Hidalgo, Washington County.

Marsh, William John
1880-1971

Composer of over 100 musical works including our state song, **Texas, Our Texas** (John P. Sousa said the finest state song he ever heard)
Buried: Greenwood Cemetery, Fort Worth.

Marshall, John Ligett
1811-1897

Veteran of the Battle of San Jacinto, 1st Regiment, Texas Volunteers, Company D
Buried: Greathouse Cemetery near Heidenhemer, Bell County.

Marshall, William
-1836

Perished defending the Alamo, March 6, 1836, at age of 28
Buried: with the Alamo heroes.

Martin, Othol "Abe"
1909-1979

Texas Sports Hall of Fame for Football, Coach at T. C. U. for many years
Buried: Fort Worth.

Martin, Albert
-1836

Captain in the Texas Army, Brought 32 men from Gonzales to help defend the Alamo; Died there at the age of 30
Buried: with the heroes of the Alamo.

Martin, Henry
-1836

Massacred as one of Fannin's men at Goliad
Buried: Goliad.

Martin, Wyly
1776-1842

Member of Austin's Old 300, Scout for William Henry Harrison, Veteran of the Battle of Horse Shoe Bend
Buried: Richmond, Texas.

Mason, Charles
1812-1883

Veteran of the Battle of Gonzales and the Battle of San Jacinto; Regular Infantry, Company A
Buried: Houston.

Mattern, Peter
-1836

Massacred as one of Fannin's men at Goliad
Buried: Goliad.

Maverick, Samuel Augustus
1803-1870

Signer of the Texas Declaration of Independence from South Carolina; Civil servant, Mayor of San Antonio
Buried: City Cemetery No. 1, San Antonio.

Maybee, Jacob
-1838

Veteran of the Battle of San Jacinto; 1st Regiment, Texas Volunteers, Company I (William Fisher's Company)
Buried: Founders' Memorial Park, Houston.

Mayo, William Leonidas
1861-1917

"Pioneer Prince of Southern Education," Power behind the founding of East Texas State Teachers College (now ETSU, not built until after his death)
Buried: on campus at ETSU.

Mays, Samuel A. J.
   -1836

Massacred as one of Fannin's men at Goliad
Buried: Goliad.

McArdle, Harry Arthur
1836-1908

Outstanding Texas artist, Professor of Art, Painted **Dawn at the Alamo** and **The Battle of San Jacinto**, Served on Gen. Robert E. Lee's staff
Buried: City Cemetery N6, San Antonio.

McCafferty, Edward
   -1836

Perished defending the Alamo, March 6, 1836, rank of lieutenant
Buried: with the heroes of the Alamo.

McCaleb, Walter Flavius
1893-1967

Historian and Writer; Works include **The Mier Expedition, Spanish Missions of Texas, The Santa Fe Expedition, The Aaron Burr Conspiracy** and 3 volumes of poetry
Buried: Mt. Calvary Cemetery, Austin.

McCallum
Jane Le Gette Yelvington
1878-1957

Writer and lecturer, Texas Secretary of State; Found and rescued the original Texas Declaration of Independence; Many civic interests and contributions
Buried: Oakwood Cemetery, Austin.

McCormick, "Frenchy"
   -1941

Gambling house operator when Tascosa was the cowboy capital of the Panhandle (late 1870's), Entertained many western bad men as well as sheriffs
Buried: Casa Romero Cemetery on Cheyenne Creek 1 mile below Tascosa.

McCormick, Joseph Manson
1806-1865

Veteran of the Battle of San Jacinto, 2nd Regiment, Texas Volunteers, 4th Company
Buried: Presbyterian Cemetery, West Columbia.

McCoy, James
   -1836

Massacred as one of Fannin's men at Goliad
Buried: Goliad.

McCoy, Jessie
   -1836

Perished defending the Alamo; One of 32 who went from Gonzales to help defend the Alamo
Buried: with the heroes of the Alamo.

McCoy, Thomas	Member of Austin's Old 300 Buried: Alleyton.
McCrocklin, Jesse Lindsay *1800-1888*	Veteran of the Battle of San Jacinto, 1st Regiment, Texas Volunteers, Company H Buried: Blanco, Texas.
McCulloch, Ben *1811-1862*	Commanders of the "Twin Sisters" (2 six-pound cannons given to Texas by the people of Cincinnati, Ohio) at the Battle of San Jacinto; Forced surrender of David Twiggs at San Antonio; Served as general in Confederate Army, Killed at the Battle of Pea Ridge Buried: State Cemetery, Austin.
McCulloch, Henry Eustace *1816-1895*	General in the Confederate Army Buried: San Geronimo Cemetery, Seguin.
McCulloch, Samuel *1810-1893*	Free Negro, His was 1st blood shed for Texas independence when he was wounded during the attack on Goliad Buried: McCulloch Cemetery near Macdona, Bexar County.
McCullough, John *1805-1870*	Presbyterian church organizer, Founded churches in San Antonio and Galveston Buried: Prairie Lea, Texas.
McDonald, James A. *-1836*	Massacred as one of Fannin's men at Goliad Buried: Goliad.
McDonald, William Jesse *1852-1918*	Sheriff, Texas Ranger, Marshal, Presidential body guard Buried: Quanah, Texas.
McDowell, William *-1836*	Perished defending the Alamo, March 6, 1836, at the age of 40 Buried: with the heroes of the Alamo.
McDonald, William Johnson *1844-1926*	Philanthropist, Gave money to erect the McDonald Observatory in the Davis Mountains of Texas

Buried: Evergreen Cemetery, Paris, Texas.

McFadin, David H.
1816-1896

Veteran of the Battle of San Jacinto, 2nd Regiment, Texas Volunteers, 3rd Company, Infantry
Buried: 2 miles below Circleville, Williamson County.

McFarland, Thomas
1810-1880

Veteran of the Siege of Bexar and Battle of Nacogdoches; Surveyed towns of San Augustine, Belgrade and Pendleton
Buried: San Augustine.

McGee, James
-1836

Perished defending the Alamo, March 6, 1836
Buried: with the heroes of the Alamo.

McGee, Richard
-1842

Killed at the Dawson Massacre
Buried: Monument Hill, LaGrange.

McGiffin, Philo Norton
1900-1964

Writer and news commentator, Political analyst, Author of historical novels, Professor of history at U. T. at Arlington
Buried: Memorial Gardens, Arlington.

McGloin, James
1801-1856

Empresario, Co-founder of a settlement known as the Irish colony
Buried: old cemetery 1.5 miles SE of San Patricio.

McGloin, John
-1836

Massacred as one of Fannin's men at Goliad
Buried: Goliad.

McGowan, Dennis
-1836

Massacred as one of Fannin's men at Goliad
Buried: Goliad.

McGowan, John
-1836

Massacred as one of Fannin's men at Goliad
Buried: Goliad.

McGregor, John
-1836

Perished defending the Alamo, March 6, 1836, at age of 34, rank of 2nd sergeant
Buried: with the heroes of the Alamo.

McGregor, Stuart Malcolm
1892-1963

Editor of the **Texas Almanac** (1925-1963), Contributor to numerous historical publications
Buried: Sparkman-Hillcrest, Dallas.

McHorse, John W.
1812-1897

Veteran of the Battle of San Jacinto; 2nd Regiment, Texas Volunteers, 1st Company
Buried: State Cemetery, Austin.

McIntire, Thomas H.
1804-1837

Veteran of the Battle of San Jacinto, 2nd Regiment, Texas Volunteers, 5th Company, Infantry
Buried: Texana, Jackson County.

McKay, Daniel
1814-1889

Veteran of the Battle of San Jacinto, 1st Regiment, Texas Volunteers Company H
Buried: Donahoe Cemetery, Bell County.

McKenzie, Kenneth
-1836

Massacred as one of Fannin's men at Goliad
Buried: Goliad.

McKinley, Charles
-1836

Massacred as one of Fannin's men at Goliad
Buried: Goliad.

McKinney, Collin
1766-1861

Helped to write the Texas Declaration of Independence, Signer of the Declaration, from New Jersey; Served in the House of Representatives of the Republic; Leader of earliest group of Disciples of Christ in Texas; Collin County named for him
Buried: Van Alstyne.

McKinney, Samuel
1807-1879

Presbyterian minister, 1st president of Austin College
Buried: near building in which Austin College was established, Huntsville.

McKinney, Robert
-1836

Perished defending the Alamo, March 6, 1836, at age of 27
Buried: with the heroes of the Alamo.

McKinney, Thomas F.
1801-1873

Member of Austin's Old 300, "Creator of the Texas Navy"
Buried: Oakwood Cemetery, Austin.

McKinstry, George B.
1802-1837

Veteran of the Battle of Velasco, Judge; Stephen F. Austin died in his home
Buried: West Columbia.

McKnight, Joseph Banning (M.D.)
1869-1961

Contributed much in the treatment of tuberculosis and the training of those dealing with the disease
Buried: San Angelo.

McLennan, Alexander
-1836

Massacred as one of Fannin's men at Goliad
Buried: Goliad.

McLeod, Hugh
1814-1861

Indian fighter, Commander of the Santa Fe Expedition, Colonel in the Confederate Army
Buried: State Cemetery, Austin.

McManomy, J. B.
-1836

Massacred as one of Fannin's men at Goliad
Buried: Goliad.

McManus, Robert Orson William
1812-1865

Veteran of the Battle of San Jacinto, 2nd Regiment, Texas Volunteers, 3rd Company, Infantry; Surveyor
Buried: State Cemetery, Austin.

McMillan, Edward
1814-1865

Veteran of the Battle of San Jacinto; 2nd Regiment, Texas Volunteers, 6th Company, Infantry
Buried: Camp Creek Cemetery, 8 miles E of Franklin.

McMillin, Alvin Nugent ("Bo")
1895-1952

Texas Sports Hall of Fame for Football, Star player and coach
Buried: Fort Worth.

McMullen, John
1785-1853

Empresario, With James McGloin founded a settlement known as the Irish colony
Buried: San Antonio.

McMurray, William
-1836

Massacred as one of Fannin's men at Goliad
Buried: Goliad.

McNeel, John

Member of Austin's Old 300
Buried: China Grove, Marion County (McNeel's Landing).

McNeel, John Greenville
1802-

Member of Austin's Old 300
Buried: Ellersby Plantation, Brazoria County.

McNeel, Pleasant, D.
1796-1871

Veteran of the Battle of San Jacinto; 1st Regiment, Texas Volunteers
Buried: Gulf Prairie, Brazoria County.

McSherry, James
-1836

Massacred as one of Fannin's men at Goliad
Buried: Goliad.

Mehang, Emma (Grigsby)
1873-1937

Texas' first female Secretary of State; Took historical documents out of storage, restored and processed them for reference and exhibition; Leader in civic, cultural, church and political affairs
Buried: Plainview.

Melton, Eliel
-1836

Perished defending the Alamo, March 6, 1836, at age of 40, rank of lieutenant — quartermaster
Buried: with the heroes of the Alamo.

Menard,
Michel Branamour
1805-1856

Signer of the Texas Declaration of Independence, from Canada
Buried: Catholic Cemetery, Galveston.

Menchaca, Jose Antonio
1800-1879

Veteran of the Siege of Bexar the Battle of San Jacinto; 2nd Regiment, Texas Volunteers, 9th Company, Infantry
Buried: San Fernando Cemetery N1, San Antonio.

Menefee, John Sutherland
1813-1884

Veteran of the Battle of San Jacinto; Moseley Baker's Company
Buried: family cemetery near Edna.

Menefee, William
1796-1875

Signer of the Texas Declaration of Independence, From Indiana
Buried: State Cemetery, Austin.

Mercer, Eli
1790-1872

Supplier of food to the Texas Army during the Revolution; Printed the **Telegraph and Texas Register** (was Gail Borden, Jr.'s father-in-law) Veteran of the Battle of San Jacinto; 1st producer of sugar in Texas; Charter trustee of Baylor University
Buried: Egypt, Texas (Wharton Co.).

Mercer, Elijah G.
1819-1856

Veteran of the Battle of San Jacinto; 1st Regiment, Texas Volunteers, Company F
Buried: Egypt, Texas (Wharton Co.).

**Merrifield,
William Jefferson**
-1836

Massacred as one of Fannin's men at Goliad
Buried: Goliad

Meusebach, John O.
1812-1897

Founder of the city of Fredericksburg, May 8, 1846
Buried: Cherry Springs, Texas.

Milam, Benjamin Rush
1788-1835

Friend of the Indians; Veteran of the War of 1812; Commander of the Texas forces storming Bexar in 1835; Killed in the assault on Verimandi's Palace on Dec. 8, 1835, at age of 44
Buried: Milam Square, San Antonio.

Millard, Henry
1807-1844

Commander of the right flank of Texas troops at the Battle of San Jacinto, Regular Infantry; Laid out city of Beaumont (named after his wife's maiden name)
Buried: Episcopal Cemetery, Galveston.

Miller, Barry
1864-1933

Judge, civil servant; Established Millermore Plantation near Dallas; Lieutenant governor of Texas
Buried: Millermore, Dallas,

Miller, Hugh
-1838

Veteran of the Battle of San Jacinto; 1st Regiment, Texas Volunteers,

Company B
Buried: Brazoria.

Miller, Isaac N.
-1836

Massacred as one of Fannin's men at Goliad
Buried: Goliad.

Miller, James M.
-1836

Massacred as one of Fannin's men at Goliad
Buried: Goliad.

Miller, Thomas R.
1795-1836

Perished defending the Alamo; One of 32 from Gonzales who went to the defense of the Alamo, at age of 41
Buried: with the heroes of the Alamo.

Millerman, Ira
1816-1887

Veteran of the Battle of San Jacinto; Artillery
Buried: Caldwell, Burleson County.

Mills, Seaborn A.
-1836

Massacred as one of Fannin's men at Goliad
Buried: Goliad.

Mills, William
-1836

Perished defending the Alamo, March 6, 1836, at age of 21
Buried: with the heroes of the Alamo.

Millsaps, Isaac
-1836

Perished defending the Alamo; One of 32 from Gonzales who went to help defend the Alamo, at age of 41
Buried: with the heroes of the Alamo.

Milne, Charles C.
-1836

Massacred as one of Fannin's men at Goliad
Buried: Goliad.

Minor, Drury Hugh
-1836

Massacred as one of Fannin's men at Goliad
Buried: Goliad.

Mitchasson, Edward F.
1807-1836

Perished defending the Alamo, March 6, 1836, at age of 29, a surgeon
Buried: with the heroes of the Alamo.

Mitchell, Asa
1795-1865

Veteran of the Battle of San Jacinto; 1st Regiment, Texas Volunteers, Company B; Member of Austin's Old

Buried: family plot near ranch home at
San Antonio.

Mitchell, Edwin T.
-1836

Perished defending the Alamo,
March 6, 1836, at age of 30
Buried: with the heroes of the Alamo.

Mitchell, Eli
1790's-1876

Veteran of the Siege of Bexar; One of
the founders of the Masonic Order in
Texas
Buried: family plot near ranch home at
San Antonio.

Mitchell, James
-1856

Veteran of the Battle of San Jacinto,
2nd Regiment, Texas Volunteers, 1st
Company, Infantry
Buried: Boonville, Brazos County.

Mitchell, Napoleon B.
-1836

Perished defending the Alamo,
March 6, 1836, at age of 32
Buried: with the heroes of the Alamo.

Mitchell, Nathaniel
1817-1897

Veteran of the Battle of San Jacinto,
1st Regiment, Texas Volunteers,
Company H
Buried: San Marcos.

**Mitchell,
Warren Jordan (M.D.)**
-1836

Massacred as one of Fannin's men at
Goliad, Brother of Edwin T. Mitchell
who died at the Alamo
Buried: Goliad.

Mitchell, Washington
-1836

Massacred as one of Fannin's men
at Goliad
Buried: Goliad.

Mixon, Claiborne D.
-1836

Massacred as one of Fannin's men
at Goliad
Buried: Goliad.

Moat, John
-1836

Massacred as one of Fannin's men
at Goliad
Buried: Goliad.

Mock, William N.
1806-1843

Veteran of the Battle of San Jacinto;
1st Regiment, Texas Volunteers,

Company D
Buried: Walker County.

Montgomery,
Edmund Duncan (M.D.)
1835-1911

Noted European doctor and scientific researcher, field of tuberculosis, Writer; Married famous sculpturess, Elizabet Ney in 1863
Buried: Liendo Plantation, Hempstead, Texas.

Montgomery, McGready
1812-1875

Veteran of the Battle of San Jacinto; Company A, Regular Infantry
Buried: Austin County.

Montgomery, Robert W.
-1837

Veteran of the Battle of San Jacinto; Henry Teal's Company
Buried: Founders' Memorial Park, Houston.

Montgomery,
Vaida Stewart
1888-1959

Poet, Publisher of the "Kaleidograph," a magazine for poets
Buried: Dallas.

Montgomery,
Whitney Maxwell
1877-1966

With his wife, Vaida, published the "Kaleidograph" (1929-1959)
Buried: Dallas.

Mood, Francis Asbury
1830-1884

Leader in Texas Methodism, One of the founders of Southwestern University
Buried: Georgetown.

Moody,
Daniel James, Jr.
1893-1966

Governor of Texas (1927-1931), Youngest governor in state's history (33 years old), Strict prison pardon policy
Buried: State Cemetery, Austin.

Moody, Edward
-1836

Massacred as one of Fannin's men at Goliad
Buried: Goliad.

Moore, David
-1836

Massacred as one of Fannin's men at Goliad
Buried: Goliad.

Moore, John H.
-1836

Massacred as one of Fannin's men at Goliad
Buried: Goliad.

Moore, John Henry
1800-1880

Member of Austin's Old 300, Commander at Battle of Gonzales, Designer of the "Come and Take It" flag, Indian fighter during Lamar's term, Confederate general from Texas, Built Moore's Fort in 1831 (later became LaGrange)
Buried: family cemetery 8 miles N of LaGrange.

Moore, John O.
-1836

Massacred as one of Fannin's men at Goliad
Buried: Goliad.

Moore, John W.
1797-1846

Signer of the Texas Declaration of Independence, from Pennsylvania
Buried: Founders' Memorial Park, Houston.

Moore, Robert B.
-1836

Perished defending the Alamo, March 6, 1836, at age of 55
Buried: with the heroes of the Alamo.

Moore, Willis A.
-1836

Perished defending the Alamo, March 6, 1836, at age of 28
Buried: with the heroes of the Alamo.

Mordoff, Henry
1817-1870

Veteran of the Battle of San Jacinto; Regular Infantry, Company B
Buried: near Smithville.

More, Robert Lee
1873-1941

Rancher, Collector of birds' eggs for over 50 years; Most outstanding private collection in the world, Ornithologist
Buried: Vernon.

Moreland, Isaac N.
1842

Veteran of the Battle of San Jacinto; Artillery
Buried: Unknown grave in Founders' Memorial Park, Houston.

Moreland, Jackson Arnot ("Peg")
1892-1973

Known state wide as a singer and composer of ballads, Member of the cast of the Early Birds show on radio for many years, Nickname came from his losing his right leg in a train accident
Buried: Plainview Cemetery, Plainview.

Morgan, John F.
-1836

Massacred as one of Fannin's men at Goliad
Buried: Goliad.

Morrell, Z. N.
1803-1883

Early Texas evangelist, Organizer of 1st regular Baptist church in the state
Buried: State Cemetery, Austin.

Morris, J. Walter
1880-1961

Texas Sports Hall of Fame for Baseball, "Mr. Baseball of the Southwest"; Organized more leagues (14) and was president of more (7) than any other person on record
Buried: Restland Cemetery, Dallas.

Moses, David
-1836

Massacred as one of Fannin's men at Goliad
Buried: Goliad.

**Mottley,
Junuis William (M.D.)**
1812-1836

Signer of the Texas Delcaration of Independence, from Virginia; On Genral Rusks's staff; Killed at the Battle of San Jacinto
Buried: on the field at San Jacinto.

Mouzon, Edwin Dubose
1869-1937

Methodist minister and bishop, Instrumental in the founding of S.M.U., Professor and 1st dean of School of Theology there, Writer
Buried: Oakland Cemetery, Dallas.

Mulkey, Abe

Evangelist, Had home across from courthouse in Corsicana
Buried: Corsicana.

Munson, Charles Rufus
-1836

Massacred as one of Fannin's men at Goliad
Buried: Goliad.

Munson, Thomas Volney
1843-1913

Botanist, Texas grape developer
Buried: Fairview Cemetery, Denison.

**Murchison,
Clinton, Williams**
1895-1969

Oilman, Founder of Southern Union Gas Company and American Liberty Oil Company
Buried: Athens, Texas.

Murdock, David A.
-1836

Massacred as one of Fannin's men at Goliad
Buried: Goliad.

Murphy, James
-1836

Killed at the Battle of Refugio in the Texas Revolution
Buried: Mt. Calvary Cemetery, Refugio.

Murphy, James B.
-1836

Killed at the Battle of Refugio in the Texas Revolution
Buried: Mt. Calvary Cemetery, Refugio.

Murphy, William S.
1844

Charge d'Affaires of the U.S. to the Republic of Texas
Buried: Episcopal Cemetery, Galveston.

**Muse,
Katie Cabell Currie**
1861-1929

Organizer of the Texas Division of the Daughters of the Confederacy (founded in 1896), Close friend of Winnie Davis, daughter of Jefferson Davis
Buried: Greenwood Cemetery, Dallas.

Musselman, Robert
-1836

Perished defending the Alamo, March 6, 1836, at age of 31 rank of sergeant
Buried: with the heroes of the Alamo.

Nail, Robert Edward
1908-1968

Playwright and director
Buried: Albany, Texas.

Nava, Andres
-1836

Perished defending the Alamo, March 6, 1836, at age of 26
Buried: with the heroes of the Alamo.

Navarro, Jose Antonio
1795-1871

Signer of the Texas Declaration of Independence (native Texan); Member of the Convention of 1836, Commissioner on the Santa Fe Expedition; Named the city of Corsicana for his father's birthplace (the Isle of Corsica)
Buried: San Fernando Cemetery N1, San Antonio.

Navarro, Nepomuceno
1811-1877

Signer of the Texas Declaration of Independence; 2nd Regiment, Texas Volunteers, 9th Company
Buried: San Fernando Cemetery N1, San Antonio.

Neal, Margie Elizabeth
1875-1971

1st woman member of the Texas Senate
Buried: Carthage.

Neff, Pat Morris
1871-1952

Governor of Texas (1921-1925), Strict prison pardon policy, Fought "Fergusonites" in the legislature; President of Baylor University
Buried: Oakwood Cemetery, Waco.

Neggan, George
-1836

Perished defending the Alamo, One of 32 from Gonzales who went to the defense of the Alamo, at age of 28
Buried: with the heroes of the Alamo.

Neill, James Clinton
1790-1845

Veteran of the Siege of Bexar and the Battle of San Jacinto, Regular artillery corps; Wounded at San Jacinto
Buried: Old Cemetery, Seguin.

Neiman, Abraham Lincoln
1875-1970

Co-founder of Neiman-Marcus Speciality Stores
Buried: Masonic Home Cemetery, Arlington, Texas.

Nelson, Andrew M.
-1836

Perished defending the Alamo, March 6, 1836, at age of 27
Buried: with the heroes of the Alamo.

Nelson, Edward
-1836

Perished defending the Alamo, March 6, 1836, at age of 20
Buried: with the heroes of the Alamo.

Nelson, George
-1836

Perished defending the Alamo, March 6, 1836, at age of 31
Buried: with the heroes of the Alamo.

Neven, Patrick
-1836

Massacred as one of Fannin's men at Goliad
Buried: Goliad.

Newton, Lewis William
1881-1965

Lecturer, scholar, writer, historian at North Texas State University
Buried: Roselawn Cemetery, Denton.

Ney, Elizabet
(Mrs. Edmund D.
Montgomery)
1833-1907

Oustanding, internationally recognized sculpturess, Many of her works in Austin, Washington and elsewhere
Buried: Liendo Plantation, Hempstead, Texas.

Nobles, Watkins
-1836

Massacred as one of Fannin's men at Goliad
Buried: Goliad.

Noland, Elijah
1804-1841

Veteran of the Battle of San Jacinton; 1st Regiment, Texas Volunteers, Company I (Capt. William S. Fisher's Company)
Buried: Founders' Memorial Park, Houston.

Noland, James
-1836

Massacred as one of Fannin's men at Goliad
Buried: Goliad.

Norris, John Franklin
1877-1952

Nationally known Baptist minister, Editor of the **Baptist Standard**, Pastor of 1st Baptist Church in Fort Worth for 44 years
Buried: Greenwood Cemetery, Fort Worth.

Northcross, James
-1836

Perished defending the Alamo, March 6, 1836, at age of 32
Buried: with the heroes of the Alamo.

Norton,
Anthony Banning
("Homer")
1896-1965

Texas Sports Hall of Fame for Football, Oustanding coach, 3 Southwest Conference championships at A&M, National champion in 1939
Buried: Forest Park Lawndale, Houston.

Norvell, Mrs. Lipscomb
1868-1962

Through her efforts and money the Old San Antonio Road was rediscovered
Buried: Beaumont.

Nowlan, James
-1836

Perished defending the Alamo, March 6, 1836, at age of 27
Buried: with the heroes of the Alamo.

Numlin, John
-1836

Massacred as one of Fannin's men at Goliad
Buried: Goliad.

O'Banion, Jennings
1816-1891

Veteran of the Battle of San Jacinto, 2nd Regiment, Texas Volunteers, 6th Company, Infantry
Buried: San Marcos.

O'Brien, David
-1977

Texas Sports Hall of Fame for Football, Heisman Trophy winner and other awards, Played for T.C.U. and the Philadelphia Eagles; Left football to enter the FBI in 1940
Buried: Fort Worth

O'Daniel, Wilbert Lee
1890-1969

Governor of Texas (1939-1941) Also senator, Golden Rule in government, Raised "old age pensions"
Buried: Hillcrest Memorial Park, Dallas.

O'Driscoll, Daniel
-1849

Veteran of the Battle of San Jacinto; Company A, Regular Infantry
Buried: Refugio County.

Ogden, James M.
-1843

Veteran of the Somervell Expedition and the Mier Expedition, drew black bean and was executed
Buried: Monument Hill, LaGrange.

Oliver, John M.
-1836

Massacred as one of Fannin's men at Goliad
Buried: Goliad.

Onderdonk, Robert Julian
1882-1922

Nationally known artist of life scenes
Buried: Alamo Masonic Cemetery, San Antonio

O'Neal, Zeno R.
-1836

Massacred as one of Fannin's men at Goliad
Buried: Goliad.

Osborn, Patrick
-1836

Massacred as one of Fannin's men at Goliad
Buried: Goliad.

Osburn, **Benjamin Franklin** *-1850*	Veteran of the Battle of San Jacinto; 1st Regiment, Texas Volunteers, Company A Buried: Fayette County.
Oswald, Lee Harvey *1939-1963*	Alleged assassin of President John F. Kennedy Buried: Rose Hill Cemetery, Fort Worth.
Ousley, George *1863-1948*	Fostered establishment of the College of Industrial Arts (now Texas Woman's University) and Arlington State College (now U.T. at Arlington) Buried: Fort Worth.
Owen, Clark L. *1808-1862*	Veteran of the Battle of San Jacinto; 1st Regiment, Kent Volunteers, 1st Company; Killed at the Battle of Shiloh in the Civil War Buried: Texana, Texas.
Owings, Robert Smith *-1836*	Massacred as one of Fannin's men at Goliad Buried: Goliad.
Pace, James Robert *1815-1876*	Veteran of the Battle of San Jacinto, 1st Regiment, Texas Volunteers, Company C Buried: Oakwood Cemetery, Austin.
Pace, Robert A. *-1836*	Massacred as one of Fannin's men at Goliad Buried: Goliad.
Paddock, Buckley B. *1844-1922*	Railroad promoter, Organizer of Fort Worth Chamber of Commerce Buried: Fort Worth
Padilla, Juan Antonio *-1839*	Empresario; Spanish and later Mexican official friendly to Texas; Joined Texas Army, Served on General Council Buried: Nacogdoches.
Pagan, George *-1836*	Perished defending the Alamo, March 6, 1836, at age of 26 Buried: with the heroes of the Alamo.

Paine, George W.
-1836

Massacred as one of Fannin's men at Goliad
Buried: Goliad.

Parker, Bonnie
1910-1934

Notorious outlaw, Partner of Clyde Barrow during 2-year crime spree
Buried: Crown Hill Cemetery, Dallas.

Parker, Christopher
-1836

Perished defending the Alamo, March 6, 1836, at age of 22
Buried: with the heroes of the Alamo.

Parker, Dickerson
1812-1844

Veteran of the Battle of San Jacinto; 2nd Regiment, Texas Volunteers, 1st Company
Buried: Parker family cemetery near Elkhart.

Parker, Elder Daniel
1781-1844

Founder of the Primitive Baptist Church in Texas
Buried: Parker family cemetery near Elkhart.

Parker, Isaac
1793-1883

Veteran of the Battle of San Jacinto; Elisha Clapps' Company
Buried: Turner Cemetery 6 miles NE of Weatherford.

Parker, Silas M.
-1836

Father of Cynthia Ann; Killed in the Comanche Indian raid (1836) in which Cynthia Ann and her brother were captured and taken to be raised by the Indians (See list of those buried outside of Texas at the back of this volume)
Buried: Fort Parker, 5 miles N of Groesbeck, Texas.

Parker, John K.
-1836

Massacred as one of Fannin's men at Goliad
Buried: Goliad.

Parker, William S.
-1836

Massacred as one of Fannin's men at Goliad
Buried: Goliad.

Parks, William
-1836

Perished defending the Alamo, March 6, 1836, at age of 31
Buried: with the heroes of the Alamo.

Parmer, Martin
1778-1850

Signer of the Texas Declaration of Independence, from Virginia; Had 4 wives and 16 children
Buried: State Cemetery, Austin.

Parr, Archie
1861-1942

Powerful political leader; Instrumental in founding of Texas A&I at Kingsville; Dean of the Texas Senate for 22 years
Buried: Parr Ranch home, Benavides.

Parr, George Berham
1901-1975

The original "Duke of Duval"; Championed the Spanish speaking people in South Texas; Very controversial political figure; Millionaire rancher
Buried: Benavides Cemetery.

Parvin, William
-1836

Massacred as one of Fannin's men at Goliad
Buried: Goliad.

Paschall, Samuel
1815-1874

Veteran of the Battle of San Jacinto; Company B, Regular Infantry
Buried: St. Vincent Catholic Cemetery, Houston.

Pate, Joe
1894-1948

Texas Sports Hall of Fame for Baseball
Buried: Fort Worth.

Pate, William H.
-1879

Veteran of the Battle of San Jacinto; 2nd Regiment, Texas Volunteers, 7th Company, Infantry
Buried: Victor Cemetery 8 miles N of DeLeon.

Patterson, Caleb Perry
1880-1971

Writer and lecturer, Taught at U.T. in Austin for 38 years, Earned 13 academic degrees
Buried: Austin Memorial Cemetery, Austin.

Patterson, James S.
1799-1879

Veteran of the Battle of San Jacinto, 1st Regiment, Texas Volunteers, Company I
Buried: Oakwood Cemetery, Austin.

Patterson, Charles
   -1836

Massacred as one of Fannin's men at Goliad
Buried: Goliad.

Patton, William Hester
1808-1842

Veteran of the Battle of Velasco, the Siege of Bexar and the Battle of San Jacinto; Aide-de-camp to Houston, Escort of Santa Anna to Washington D.C.
Buried: at his home 35 miles S of San Antonio.

Payne, Leon Roger
1917-1969

Nationally known country-western composer and singer, was blind
Buried: Sunset Memorial Park, San Antonio.

**Payne,
Leonidas Warren, Jr.**
1873-1945

Educator, Author, Illustrious in Texas letters; With John Lomax established the Texas Folklore Society
Buried: Oakwood Cemetery, Austin.

Pearce, James Edwin
1868-1938

Educator, Founded department of anthropology at U.T. in Austin in 1919; 1st director of the Texas Memorial Museum when it opened in 1938
Cremated, San Antonio.

Pease, Elisha Marshall
1812-1883

Governor of Texas (1853-1855, 1855-1857), New capitol building, Railroad construction, Eleemosynary institutions established; Reconstruction governor (1867-1869; Veteran of the Battle of Gonzales; Distinguished early Texas Ranger
Buried: Oakwood Cemetery, Austin.

**Pease,
Julia Maria ("Miss Julia")**
1853-1918

Civic minded philanthropist, Patron of Elizabet Ney's work and other art forms; 2nd of 3 daughters of Gov. and Mrs. Pease
Buried: Oakwood Cemetery, Austin.

Peck, Nicholas
   -1863

Veteran of the Battle of San Jacinto, 1st Regiment, Texas Volunteers, Company D
Buried: Gonzales.

Peerson, Cleng
1782-1865

Father of Norse immigration to Texas (1850); Established a number of Norse settlements in the Great Lakes region (beginning 1821); Inscription on his tombstone: "Erected to his memory by grateful countrymen"
Buried: Norse, Bosque County.

Pendleton, John Wesley
-1842

Killed at the Dawson Massacre
Buried: Monument Hill, LaGrange.

Penick, Daniel Allen
1869-1964

Texas Sports Hall of Fame for Tennis, Coach, Scholar; Taught New Testament Greek at U.T. in Austin for many years; President of Texas Tennis Association for over 50 years
Buried: Oakwood Cemetery, Austin.

Penington, Sydney O.
1809-1837

Signer of the Texas Declaration of Independence, from Kentucky; Veteran of the Siege of Bexar
Buried: Shelbyville, Texas.

Penny, George W.
-1836

Massacred as one of Fannin's men at Goliad
Buried: Goliad.

Pennybacker, Anna (Mrs. Percy V. Pennybacker)
1861-1938

Early Texas educator, Wrote a textbook on Texas History which became the standard (1888)
Buried: Oakwood Cemetery, Austin.

Perkins, Austin
-1836

Massacred as one of Fannin's men at Goliad
Buried: Goliad.

Perkins, D. A. J.
-1836

Massacred as one of Fannin's men at Goliad
Buried: Goliad.

Perkins, Joseph J.
1874-1960

Oilman and rancher, Lay church leader, philanthropist
Buried: Perkins Mausoleum, Wichita Falls.

Perry,
Emily Margaret
Austin Bryan
1795-1851

Sister of Stephen F. Austin, Mother of 4 sons prominent in Texas History, Inscription on her tombstone: "Rise up and call her blessed"
Buried: Peach Point Plantation between Brazoria and Freeport.

Perry,
Holly Ballenger Bryan
1868-1955

Co-founder, with Betty Ballenger, of the Daughters of the Republic of Texas; Grandniece of Stephen F. Austin; Daughter of Guy Morrison Bryan
Buried: State Cemetery, Austin.

Perry, Louis Clausiel
1877-1926

Educator, Founder of Texas Military College in Terrell (1915) Buried: Terrell.

Perry, Richardson
-1836

Perished defending the Alamo, March 6, 1836, at age of 19
Buried: with the heroes of the Alamo.

Petrussewiez A. Adolph
-1836

Massacred as one of Fannin's men at Goliad
Buried: Goliad.

Pettus, John Freeman
1808-1878

Veteran of the Battle of San Jacinto; 1st Regiment, Texas Volunteers, Company D; Member of Austin's Old 300
Buried: Charco, Goliad County.

Pettus, Samuel Overton
-1836

Massacred as one of Fannin's men at Goliad
Buried: Goliad.

Pettus, Willam
1787-1844

Member of Austin's Old 300
Buried: Washington-on-the-Brazos.

Petty, George Washington
1812-1901

Veteran of the Battle of San Jacinto; 1st Regiment, Texas Volunteers, Company H
Buried: Prairie Lea Cemetery, Brenham.

Petty, Rufus R.
-1836

Massacred as one of Fannin's men at Goliad
Buried: Goliad.

Peyton, Jonathan C.
-1834

Member of Austin's Old 300; 1st husband of Angeline Belle Eberly
Buried: San Felipe.

Phelps, James Aeneas E.
-1847

Member of Austin's Old 300; Surgeon at the Battle of San Jacinto; Organized Masonic lodges in Texas
Buried: Orozimbo Plantation 12 miles NW of Columbia.

Phelps, Charles
-1836

Massacred as one of Fannin's men at Goliad
Buried: Goliad.

Pickens, Lucy Holcombe
1832-1899

"Lady Lucy, Queen of the Confederacy," Her picture on CSA money; Wife of U.S. ambassador to Russia, A favorite of Catherine the Second and godmother to Catherine's daughter
Buried: family cemetery, Edgewood.

Pierce, Abel Head ("Shanghai")

Cattleman, Rancher, Breeder (imported first Brahmas to Texas), Railroad builder, Banker
Buried: Hawley's Cemetery near Blessing, Texas, N of Corpus Christi.

Pierce, Stephen
-1836

Massacred as one of Fannin's men at Goliad
Buried: Goliad.

Pilgrim, Thomas J.

Founder of the first Sunday School in Texas; Tutor of Stephen Austin's nephew
Buried: City Cemetery, Gonzales.

Pittman, James F.
-1836

Massacred as one of Fannin's men at Goliad
Buried: Goliad.

Pittman, Samuel C.
-1836

Massacred as one of Fannin's men at Goliad
Buried: Goliad.

Plaster, Thomas Phiney
-1861

Veteran of the Battle of San Jacinto Artillery; Manned one of the "Twin Sisters"
Buried: State Cemetery, Austin.

Poe, George Washington
1800-1844

Veteran of the Battle of San Jacinto
Buried: Red River, Montague County.

Polancio, Jose Maria
-1855

Guide, Killed by Indians
Buried: Guadalupe Canyon, off U.S. Highway 62.

Polland, Amos (M.D.)
1803-1836

Chief surgeon at the Siege of the Alamo, Perished with the other defenders, at age of 33
Buried: with the heroes of the Alamo.

Polley, Joseph Henry
1795-1869

Member of Austin's Old 300
Buried: family plot at Stone Mansion near Sutherland Springs.

Ponton, Andrew

Veteran of the Battle of Gonzales; On Feb. 23, 1836, Travis sent Ponton an appeal asking for help — 32 from Gonzales answered
Buried: old cemetery, Gonzales.

Porter, Katherine Anne
1890-1976

Novelist of international fame; Winner of Guggenheim Fellowship (1930); Among her more famous works: **Ship of Fools** and **Pale Horse, Pale Rider**
Buried: Indian Creek Cemetery, Brownwood.

Potter, Robert
-1842

Signer of the Texas Declaration of Independence, from North Carolina; Ad interim Secretary of the Navy; Body never recovered from dive into Caddo Lake.

Powell, Lewis
-1836

Massacred as one of Fannin's men at Goliad
Buried: Goliad.

Power, James
1788-1852

Signer of the Texas Declaration of Independence, from Ireland, Empresario, Partner with James Hewetson
Buried: Mt. Calvary Cemetery, Refugio.

Powers, John M.
-1836

Massacred as one of Fannin's men at Goliad
Buried: Goliad.

Prather, **William Lambdin** *1848-1905*	Nationally recognized educator, Orignator of the phrase "The eyes of Texas are upon you"; Attended Washington College while Lee was its president, Was pall bearer at Lee's funeral; President of U.T. in Austin (1899-1905) Buried: Waco.
Pressler, Charles William *1823-1907*	Expert Texas map maker Buried: Oakwood Cemetery, Austin.
Preusch, William G. *-1836*	Massacred as one of Fannin's men at Goliad Buried: Goliad.
Pryor, Ike T. *1852-1937*	Trail Driver, Veteran Trail boss and ranchman Buried: Mission Burial Park, San Antonio.
Pryor, William *-1833*	Member of Austin's Old 300; Travis attended his funeral Buried: San Felipe.
Rabb, John *1798-1861*	Member of Austins' Old 300 Buried: Oakwood Cemetery, Austin.
Rabb, Thomas J. *-1841*	Member of Austin's Old 300 Buried: Egypt, Texas.
Raguet, Anna W. *1819-1883*	Courted by Sam Houston in 1833-1837, She did not believe his divorce from Eliza Allen was legal; refused his proposal. Buried: Raguet lot, Marshall, Texas.
Raimey, Robert R. *-1836*	Massacred as one of Fannin's men at Goliad Buried: Goliad.
Raines, Cadwell Walton *1839-1906*	Judge, Publisher, Began modern effort toward a State Library in 1891 Buried: Round Rock.

Ramsdell,
Charles William, Jr.
1877-1942

Texas Historian and Writer, Professor at U.T. in Austin, "Dean of Southern Historians"
Buried: San Antonio.

Randall, Edward (M.D.)
1860-1944

Guiding spirit of the medical branch of the University of Texas for more than 50 years
Buried: Episcopal Cemetery, Galveston.

Randolph, William M.
-1928

Captain in the U.S. Army Air Corps, Fighter pilot, Randolph Field in San Antonio named for him
Buried: San Antonio.

Rankin,
Frederic Harrison
1795-1874

Member of Austin's Old 300
Buried: Myrtle Cemetery, Ennis.

Rankin, Melinda
1811-1888

Early, avid Protestant missionary in Texas
Buried: Bloomington, IL.

Rayburn,
Samuel Taliaferro
1882-1961

Texas legislator, congressman and Speaker of the House of Representatives, 48 years of continuous service, Served under six U.S. Presidents
Buried: Willow Wild Cemetery, Bonham.

Reagin, John Henninger
1818-1905

Postmaster General of the Confederacy, Public servant
Buried: East Hill Cemetery, Palestine.

Reaugh,
Charles Franklin (Frank)
1866-1945

Nationally known artist, Painted mostly western scenes
Buried: Terrell.

Rector, Claiborne
1802-1873

Veteran of the Battle of San Jacinto, 2nd Regiment, Texas Volunteers, 4th Company, Infantry
Buried: Lavernia, Wilson County.

Rector, Pendleton
1808-1888

Veteran of the Battle of San Jacinto, 2nd Regiment, Texas Volunteers, 4th Company, Infantry
Buried: Prairie Lea Cemetery, Brenham.

Red, Samuel Clark (M.D.)
1861-1940

1st student to receive BA from University of Texas, Established 1st hospital in Houston, Introduced ambulance service in Houston, 1st to use X-ray in Houston in surgery, 1st to use diptheria antitoxin
Buried: Houston.

Red, William Stuart
1857-1933

Presbyterian minister, educator and writer
Buried: Austin.

Redd, William Davis
1810-1840

Veteran of the Battle of San Jacinto, 2nd Regiment, Texas Volunteers, Company J. Cavalry, Killed in a duel
Buried: San Antonio.

**Redman,
William Columbus**
1853-1924

Pioneer West Texas journalist
Buried: Abilene

Reed, Henry
1800-1854

Veteran of the Battle of San Jacinto; 2nd Regiment, Texas Volunteers, 8th Company, Infantry
Buried: 6 miles E of Calvert, Texas.

Reed, Isaac
-1848

Pioneer Baptist minister
Buried: Old Bethel Churchyard 3 miles W of Clayton, Panola County.

Reed, James
-1836

Massacred as one of Fannin's men at Goliad
Buried: Goliad.

Reese, Charles Keller
1810-1858

Veteran of the Siege of Bexar, the Battle of San Jacinto, the Sommervell Expedition and the Mier Expedition; 1st Regiment, Texas Volunteers, Company K
Buried: at home on Cedar Lake, Brazoria County.

Reese, Perry
-1836

Massacred as one of Fannin's men at Goliad
Buried: Goliad.

Reese, Thomas B
-1836

Massacred as one of Fannin's men at Goliad
Buried: Goliad.

Reeves, James Travis
1923-1964

Country western singer
Buried: 4 miles E of Carthage Texas, off U.S. Highway 79.

Reeves, Thomas
-1836

Massacred as one of Fannin's men at Goliad
Buried: Goliad.

Reiersen, Johan Reinert
1810-1864

Founder of a Norwegan colony in Van Zandt and Kaufman Counties in 1846, Established village of Prairieville
Buried: 4 Mile Lutheran Cemetery, Prairieville.

Reiter, Max
1905-1950

Symphony conductor, Founder of the Waco and San Antonio Symphonies, Personal friend of Richard Strauss, Guest conductor of NBC Symphony
Buried: San Antonio.

Reverchon, Julien
1837-1905

Nationally recognized botanist, Writer
Buried: in old French Cemetery near site of La Reunion colony, Dallas.

Reynolds, Carl Nettles
-1978

Texas Sports Hall of Fame for Baseball
Buried: Houston.

Reynolds, John Purdy
-1836

Perished defending the Alamo, March 6, 1836, at the age of 29.
Buried: with the heroes of the Alamo.

Rice, Thomas
-1842

Killed at the Dawson Massacre
Buried: Monument Hill, LaGrange.

Rice, William Marsh
1816-1900

Rice Institute (now Rice University) founded at his bequest; Murdered in New York City
Buried: Ashes under his statue on Rice campus, Houston.

Richards, John
-1836

Massacred as one of Fannin's men at Goliad
Buried: Goliad.

Richardson, Daniel Long
-1849

Veteran of the Battle of San Jacinto; Company A, Regular Infantry
Buried: Sabine County.

Richardson, John
-1840

Veteran of the Battle of San Jacinto; 2nd Regiment, Texas Volunteers, 6th Company, Infantry
Buried: Founders' Memorial Park, Houston.

Richardson, Sid Williams
1891-1959

1st oil producer in Fort Worth, Cattleman, Owned Texas State Network (radio); Confidante of FDR, Helped persuade Dwight Eisenhower to run for President; Philanthropist
Buried: Athens, Texas.

Richardson, Stephen
1794-1860

Member of Austin's Old 300
Buried: Houston.

Richardson, Willard
1802-1875

Journalist, Publisher of the **Galveston News**, He issued the 1st issue of **Texas Almanac**; Built 1st opera house in Galveston
Buried: Episcopal Cemetery, Galveston.

Rickard, George L. (Tex)

Texas Sports Hall of Fame for Boxing
Buried: New York City.

Riddell, Samuel
-1836

Massacred as one of Fannin's men at Goliad
Buried: Goliad.

Riddle, Joseph P.
-1836

Massacred as one of Fannin's men at Goliad
Buried: Goliad.

Ritter,
Woodward Maurice ("Tex")
1905-1974

"America's most beloved cowboy," Country western singer, Motion picture star
Buried: Oak Bluff Memorial Park, Port Neches.

Roberts, Christopher
-1843

Victim of the Mier Expedition
Buried: Monument Hill, LaGrange.

Roberts, John S.
1796-1871

Signer of the Texas Declaration of Independence, from Virginia

Buried: Oak Grove Cemetery, Nacogdoches.

Roberts, Oran Milo
1815-1898

Governor of Texas (1879-1883), New capitol building in exchange for 3,050,000 acres XIT ranch, Writer of history
Buried: Oakwood Cemetery, Austin.

Roberts, Thomas H.
-1836

Massacred as one of Fannin's men at Goliad
Buried: Goliad.

Roberts, Thomas H.
-1836

Perished defending the Alamo, March 6, 1836.

Robison, Andrew

Member of Austin's Old 300
Buried: Washington-on-the-Brazos.

Robertson, James
-1836

Perished defending the Alamo, March 6, 1836, at age of 32.

Robertson, Sterling Clack
1785-1842

Signer of the Texas Declaration of Independence, from Tennessee, Empresario
Buried: State Cemetery, Austin.

Robinson, Issac
-1836

Perished defending the Alamo, March 6, 1836, at age of 31.
Buried: with the heroes of the Alamo.

Robinson, James W.
1800-

Veteran of San Jacinto, Cavalry Company
Buried: San Diego, CA.

Robeson, Joel Walter
1815-1889

Veteran of the Battle of Velasco, the Siege of Bexar, the Battle of Concepcion and the Battle of San Jacinto; 1st Regiment, Texas Volunteers, Company F, Heard's Company; One of the men who captured Santa Anna
Buried: State Cemetery, Austin.

Rodgers, J. B.
-1836

Killed at the Battle of Refugio in the Texas Revolution
Buried: Mt. Calvary Cemetery, Refugio.

Roehm, Johan Conrad
1822-1902

Early Lutheran missionary to Texas, Founder of many churches
Buried: Galveston Cemetery.

Rogers, Samuel C. A.
1810-1892

Pioneer Methodist minister, Indian fighter, Veteran of the Siege of Bexar and the Grass Fight
Buried: Rogers family cemetery, Ganado, Jackson County.

Rooney, Cornelius
-1836

Massacred as one of Fannin's men at Goliad
Buried: Goliad.

Rose, Gideon
-1836

Massacred as one of Fannin's men at Goliad
Buried: Goliad.

Rose, James M.
-1836

Perished defending the Alamo, March 6, 1836, at the age of 33.
Buried: with the heroes of the Alamo.

Rose, Louis Moses
1785-1857

Left the Alamo on March 5, 1836, but gave the world Travis' speech, the line drawing episode, etc.; Later ran a butcher shop in Nacogdoches
Buried: Greenhill Cemetery, Mount Pleasant.

Rose, Victor Marion
1841 or 2-1893

Poet, Editor, Historian, Soldier
Buried: Evergreen Cemetery, Victoria.

Rosenberg, Henry
1824-1893

Banker, Philanthropist, Founder of an orphans' home, Civic leader in Galveston, City of Rosenberg named for him
Buried: Loudon Park Cemetery, Baltimore, MD.

Ross, James
-1849

Member of Austin's Old 300
Buried: Washington-on-the-Brazos.

Ross, Lawrence Sullivan
1838-1898

Governor of Texas (1887-1891), Capitol building completed, Prohibition defeated; Texas Ranger; Educator
Buried: Oakwood Cemetery, Waco.

Routh, Eugene Coke
1874-1966

Outstanding religious journalist
Buried: Laurel Land Memorial Park, Dallas.

Routt, Joseph D.
1914-1944

Texas Sports Hall of Fame for Football, Played for Texas A&M; Killed during the Battle of the Bulge, WWII
Buried: American Cemetery in Holland, later moved to Prairie Lea Cemetery, Brenham.

Rowan, William N.
-1843

Victim of the Mier Expedition
Buried: Monument Hill, LaGrange.

Rowe, Samuel
-1836

Massacred as one of Fannin's men at Goliad
Buried: Goliad.

**Ruby, Jack
(Jake Rubenstein)**
1911-1967

Assissinator of Lee Harvey Oswald (November 24, 1963)
Buried: Westlawn Cemetery, Chicago.

Ruiz, Jose Francisco
1783-1840

Signer of the Texas Declaration of Independence, from Texas; Alcalde of San Antonio
Buried: San Fernando Church, San Antonio.

Rumley, Thomas
-1836

Massacred as one of Fannin's men at Goliad
Buried: Goliad.

Runnels, Hardin Richard
1820-1873

Governor of Texas (1857-1859), Only person to defeat Sam Houston
Buried: State Cemetery, Austin.

Rusk, Jackson J.
-1836

Perished defending the Alamo, March 6, 1836
Buried: with the heroes of the Alamo.

Rusk, Thomas Jefferson
1803-1857

Signer of the Texas Declaration of Independence, from South Carolina; Veteran of the Battle of San Jacinto; Rank of general; Senator from Texas, Secretary of War
Buried: Oak Grove Cemetery, Nacogdoches.

Russell, Robert B.
1817-1880

Veteran of the Battle of San Jacinto, 2nd Regiment, Texas Volunteers, Texas Volunteers, 7th Company, Infantry
Buried: cemetery in Orange, Texas.

Ruter, Martin
1785-1838

"Father of Texas Methodisim," superintendent of Methodist Missions in Texas, President of Transylvania University, Instrumental in founding of Ruterville College near LaGrange
Buried: Navasota.

Rutherford, Joseph
-1836

Perished defending the Alamo, March 6, 1836, at age of 38
Buried: with the heroes of the Alamo.

Ryan, Edward
-1836

Massacred as one of Fannin's men at Goliad
Buried: Goliad.

Ryan, Isaac
-1836

Perished defending the Alamo, March 6, 1836, at age of 24
Buried: with the heroes of the Alamo.

Sadler, John
1808-1885

2nd Regiment, Texas Volunteers, 2nd Company
Buried: Kosse, Limestone County.

Sadler, William Turner
1801-1883

Veteran of the Battle of San Jacinto; 2nd Regiment, Texas Volunteers, 1st Company, Infantry
Buried: Sadler Cemetery 12 miles NE of Grapeland.

Sager, Christopher Adam
1826-1869

One of the 1st two Lutheran pastors in Texas
Buried: Arncekeville, Texas.

Salmon, Richard
1797-1849

Episcopal priest in Texas, Officiated at the funeral of Stephen F. Austin; Died of cholera near Baton Rouge, Louisiana
Buried: family cemetery, Wise County.

Samuell, W. W. (M.D.)
1878-1937

Prominent Dallas County physician and philanthropist
Buried: Sparkman-Hillcrest Mausoleum, Dallas.

Sanders, John
1816-1871

Veteran of the Battle of San Jacinto, Company A, Regular Infantry
Buried: Center, Texas.

Sanders, Samuel Smith
-1836

Massacred as one of Fannin's men at Goliad
Buried: Goliad.

Sanders, Wade H.
-1836

Massacred as one of Fannin's men at Goliad
Buried: Goliad.

Sanger, Alexander
1847-1925

President of Sanger Brothers Department Stores, Civic leader
Buried: Emanuel Cemetery, Dallas.

Sargent, Charles
-1836

Massacred as one of Fannin's men at Goliad
Buried: Goliad.

Saunders, Bacon (M.D.)
1855-1925

Performed first successful operation for acute appendicitis in Texas, Professor of surgery at Baylor Medical College, President of Texas Medical Association
Buried: Fort Worth.

Saunders, James H.
-1836

Massacred as one of Fannin's men at Goliad
Buried: Goliad.

Savage, William
-1842

Killed at the Dawson Massacre
Buried: Monument Hill, LaGrange.

Sayers, Joseph Draper
1841-1929

Governor of Texas (1899-1903), Independent school districts began, Poll taxes, Eleemonsynary institutions added
Buried: Bastrop.

Sayle, Antoine
-1836

Killed at the Battle of Refugio in the Texas Revolution
Buried: Mt. Calvary Cemetery, Refugio.

Scallorn, Elam
-1842

Killed at the Dawson Massacre
Buried: Monument Hill, LaGrange.

Scates, William Bennett
1802-1882

Signer of the Texas Declaration of Independence, from Virginia; Veteran of the Battle of Velasco, the Siege of Bexar and the Battle of San Jacinto; 2nd Regiment, Texas Volunteers, 1st Company, Infantry
Buried: State Cemetery, Austin.

Schott, Justus J.
1846-1928

Early experimenter with chewing gum chicle (before Adams), added sugar and flavoring refining; Won case against Adams but did not pursue
Buried: Hallettsville.

**Schreiner,
Gustave Frederick**
1866-1962

"Dean of the Hill Country Ranchers," Land and Livestock Company, Philanthropic to Schreiner Institute established by his father, Charles A. Schreiner
Buried: Kerrville.

Schreiner, Louis Albert
1870-1970

Banker, Philanthropist, Brother of Gustave Frederick
Buried: Kerrville.

Schultz, Henry Lewis
-1836

Massacred as one of Fannin's men at Goliad
Buried: Goliad.

Scott, Arthur Carroll (M.D.)
1865-1940

Internally recognized physician, Co-founder of Scott & White Hospital in Temple (largest private hospital in the Southwest)
Buried: Hillcrest Cemetery, Temple.

Scott, James
1816-1868

Member of Austin's Old 300
Buried: Houston.

Scott, R. J.
-1836

Massacred as one of Fannin's men at Goliad
Buried: Goliad.

Scott, William T.

Pioneer statesman and industrial developer of Texas
Buried: family cemetery, Scottsville, 8 miles E of Marshall.

Scott,
Zachary Thomson (M.D.)
1880-1964

Leader in the treatment of TB, Instituted sale of TB seals in Texas
Buried: Memorial Park, Austin.

Scott,
Zachary Thomson, Jr.
1914-1965

Broadway actor, Hollywood star, TV personality
Buried: Memorial Park, Austin.

Scurlock, Mial
1809-1836

Veteran of the Siege of Bexar, Perished defending the Alamo, March 6, 1836, age of 27
Buried: with the heroes of the Alamo.

Scurlock, William
1807-1885

Veteran of the Grass Fight, the Matamoras Expedition (escaped), the Agua Dulce Creek (escaped, and the Coleto Creek Battle (escaped)
Buried: San Augustine.

Scurry, Richardson A.
1811-1862

Veteran of the Battle of San Jacinto, Artillery; Legislator, Lawyer
Buried: Hempstead.

Seale,
Richard ("Uncle Dick")
1797?-1875

Founder of the oldest Negro church in Texas (1850?): Dixie Baptist Church for Negroes where he was first pastor
Buried: Seale cemetery, Indian Creek W of Jasper.

Sealy, John
1822-1884

Organized Galveston Gas Company; President of the Santa Fe Railroad; Bequeathed part of his estate to found a hospital open to all regardless of ability to pay (Erected in Galveston in 1887)
Buried: Galveston.

Sealy, John
-1836

Massacred as one of Fannin's men at Goliad
Buried: Goliad.

Seaton, J. M.
-1836

Massacred as one of Fannin's men at Goliad
Buried: Goliad.

Secrest, Fielding G.
-1854

Veteran of the Battle of San Jacinto; 2nd Regiment, Texas Volunteers under Karnes, With group capturing Santa

Anna
Buried: Columbus.

Seguin, Erasmo
1782-1857

One of the first in Texas to experiment with growing cotton; 1st alcalde of Bexar, Close friend and helper of Stephen F. Austin; Died at his ranch 33 miles from San Antonio.

Seguin, Juan Nepomuceno
1806-1890

An independence figure who at one time was considered a traitor by both Texas and Mexico; Travis' courier from Alamo to colonies
Buried: Seguin, Texas.

Seguin, Juan Nepomuceno

Veteran of the Battle of San Jacinto
Buried: Santiago, Mexico.

Selectman, Charles Claude
1874-1958

Methodist minister and bishop, President of S. M. U.
Buried: Sparkman-Hillcrest Cemetery, Dallas.

Self, George
-1856

Veteran of the Battle of San Jacinto; 1st Regiment, Texas Volunteers, Company C (Gene Billingsly's company) Buried: Manor Cemetery, near Webberville, Travis County.

Selman, John
-1896

Killed John Wesley Hardin, Was killed by a U.S. marshal
Buried: El Paso.

Sevenman, Frederick
-1836

Massacred as one of Fannin's men at Goliad
Buried: Goliad.

Seward, John
-1836

Massacred as one of Fannin's men at Goliad
Buried: Goliad.

Sewell, Marcus L.
-1836

Perished defending the Alamo, March 6, 1836, at age of 31
Buried: with the heroes of the Alamo.

Shackleford, Fortunatus S.
-1836

Massacred as one of Fannin's men at Goliad
Buried: Goliad.

Shackelford, William J.
-1836

Massacred as one of Fannin's men at Goliad
Buried: Goliad.

Sharp, John
-1840

Veteran of the Battle of San Jacinto, 1st Regiment, Texas Volunteers, Company K
Buried: Velasco.

Sharp, Walter Benona
1870-1912

Outstanding figure in the oil industry industry in Texas, Personal friend and associate investor with Howard Hughes, One of the developers of Roller Rock bit, Founder of what would become Texaco
Buried: Houston.

Shaw, James
1808-1879

Veteran of the Battle of San Jacinto; 2nd Regiment, Texas Volunteers, Company J, Cavalary
Buried: Early Chapel Cemetery, Lexington, Texas.

Shearer, Gordon Kent
1880-1971

Leading newspaper man, With UP in Austin for 20 years, Gave Walter Cronkite his early training
Buried: Memorial Park, Austin.

Shelby, David
1799-1872

Member of Austin's Old 300
Buried: Shelby, Austin County.

Shelton, William
-1836

Killed at the Battle of Refugio in the Texas Revolution
Buried: Mt. Calvary Cemetery, Refugio.

Sheppard, Morris
1875-1941

U. S. Congressman and Senator (1913-1941), Introduced the 18th Amendment
Buried: Texarkana.

Shepherd, J. L.
-1843

Member of the Mier Expedition, Drew a black bean and was executed
Buried: Monument Hill, LaGrange.

Sheridan, Ann
(Clara Lou Sheridan)
1915-1967

Famous movie and television star, From Denton
Buried: Hollywood, CA.

Sherman, Sidney
1805-1873

Veteran of the Battle of San Jacinto, 2nd Regiment, Texas Volunteers Comander
Buried: Lakeview Cemetery, Galveston.

Shettles, Elijah L.
1852-1940

A leader in the Methodist Church in Texas, Writer, Collector of books given to S. M. U. and U. T.
Buried: Oakwood Cemetery, Austin.

Shied, Manson
-1836

Perished defending the Alamo, March 6, 1836, at age of 25
Buried: with the heroes of the Alamo.

Shipman, Daniel
1801-1881

Member of Austin's Old 300
Buried: State Cemetery, Austin.

Short, Luke
1854-1893

"Best dresser, best shot and best gambler in Fort Worth," Friend of Wyatt Earp
Buried: Oakwood Cemetery, Fort Worth.

Short, Walter Campbell
1880-1949

Major general, U. S. Army, at Pearl Harbor, December 7, 1941, "Scapegoat" of sneak attack
Buried: Arlington National Cemetery.

Short, Zachariah H.
-1836

Massacred as one of Fannin's men at Goliad
Buried: Goliad.

Shotwell, Pete
-1978

Texas Sports Hall of Fame for Football, Long time Texas coach and player
Buried: Elmwood Cemetery, Abilene.

Shuler, Ellis W.
-1954

Geologist, Teacher, 1st chairman of Department of Geology at S. M. U.
Buried: Restland Park, Dallas.

Sikes, J. V.
-1964

Texas Sports Hall of Fame for Football, Coach
Buried: Commerce.

Simmons, Cleveland K.
-1836

Perished defending the Alamo, March 6, 1836, at age of 26, lieutenant of cavalry
Buried: with the heroes of the Alamo.

Simmons, S.
-1836

Massacred as one of Fannin's men at Goliad
Buried: Goliad.

Simpson, Lawson S.
-1836

Massacred as one of Fannin's men at Goliad
Buried: Goliad.

Simpson, William N.
-1836

Massacred as one of Fannin's men at Goliad
Buried: Goliad.

Simpson,
-1836

Killed at the Battle of Refugio in the Texas Revolution
Buried: Mt. Calvary Cemetery, Refugio.

Simms, Thomas
-1842

Killed at the Dawson Massacre
Buried: Monument Hill, LaGrange.

Slack, Richard
-1842

Killed at the Dawson Massacre
Buried: Monument Hill, LaGrange.

Slatter, Randolph
-1836

Massacred as one of Fannin's men at Goliad
Buried: Goliad.

Slaughter, Christopher Columbus
1837-1919

Cattleman, Trail driver, Millionaire philanthropist
Buried: Greenwood Mausoleum, Dallas.

Smith, A. Frank
1889-1962

Methodist minister and bishop, In charge of all missionary work of church for 20 years, Organized Highland Park Methodist Church, Dallas
Buried: Forest Park-Lawndale Cemetery, Houston.

Smith, Andrew H.
-1836

Perished defending the Alamo, March 6, 1836, at age of 21
Buried: with the heroes of the Alamo.

Smith, Ashbel, (M.D.)
1805-1886

Surgeon general of Texas Army as of 1837, Texas minister in Washington,

Educator, Civil servant and friend of Texas
Buried: State Cemetery, Austin.

Smith, Charles S.
-1836

Perished defending the Alamo,
March 6, 1836, at age of 30
Buried: with the heroes of the Alamo.

Smith, Erastus ("Deaf")
1787-1837

Principal scout for Sam Houston during the Texas Revolution; 2nd Regiment, Texas Volunteers, Cavalry
Buried: Richmond, Texas.

Smith, Mrs. Erastus

Buried: Catholic Cemetery, San Antonio.

Smith, Gavin H.
-1836

Killed at the Battle of Refugio in the Texas Revolution
Buried: Mt. Calvary Cemetery, Refugio.

Smith, Henry
1788-1851

Veteran of the Battle of San Jacinto; Early leader of the War Party; Provisional governor (1835-1836); Defeated in try for office of President of Texas (1836); Died in a mining camp in Los Angeles County, California.

Smith, James
-1836

Massacred as one of Fannin's men at Goliad
Buried: Goliad.

Smith, John
-1843

Veteran of the Battle of San Jacinto, Regular Infantry
Buried: Montgomery County.

Smith, John H.
-1843

Veteran of the Battle of San Jacinto; Company A, Regular Infantry
Buried: Harris County.

Smith, John W.
1801-1845

Guide for the 32 who went from Gonzales to help defend the Alamo; Carried Travis' letter to the President of the Convention on March 3, 1836; Mayor of San Antonio (1837)
Buried: San Antonio.

Smith, John William
1792-1845

Veteran of the Battle of Concepcion and the Siege of Bexar; Carried the last

dispatch out of the Alamo
Buried: State Park, Washington-on-the-Brazos.

Smith, Joshua G.
-1836

Perished defending the Alamo, March 6, 1836, at the age of 28
Buried: with the heroes of the Alamo.

Smith, Robert W.
1814-1851

Veteran of the Battle of San Jacinto, Hayden Arnold's Company, Fired the shot that killed Chief Bowles
Buried: Pleasant Hill Cemetery 7 miles W of Henderson.

Smith, Sydney
-1836

Massacred as one of Fannin's men at Goliad
Buried: Goliad.

Smith, William A.
-1836

Massacred as one of Fannin's men at Goliad
Buried: Goliad.

Smith, William H.
-1836

Perished defending the Alamo, March 6, 1836, at age of 27
Buried: with the heroes of the Alamo.

Smithwick, Noah
1808-1899

Veteran of the Battle of Concepcion; Texas Ranger; Published **The Evolution of a State**
Died in Santa Ana, California.

Smyth, George Washington
1803-1866

Signer of the Texas Declaration of Independence, from North Carolina
Buried: State Cemetery, Austin.

Snively, Jacob
1809-1871

Rank of colonel, Leader of the Snively Expedition, Prospector and Miner; Killed by Indians
Buried: Gillette, AZ.

Sparks, Stephen F.
1819-1908

Veteran of the Battle of San Jacinto, 2nd Regiment, 1st Company, Infantry; Last president of the Texas Veterans Association
Buried: Rockport.

Speaker,
Tristram E. ("Tris")
1888-1958

First athlete named to the Texas Sports Hall of Fame; Famous baseball player and manager, 22 years in the major leagues, Lifetime batting average of .344
Buried: Fairview Cemetery, Hubbard.

Speck, Hugo T.
1906-1970

AP war correspondent, Chief of INS in Germany, Personally knew Hitler and Mussolini
Buried: Restland Park, Dallas.

Spencer, Henry
-1836

Massacred as one of Fannin's men at Goliad
Buried: Goliad.

Sprague, Samuel
-1836

Massacred as one of Fannin's men at Goliad
Buried: Goliad.

St. Denis,
Louis Juchereau de
1676-1744

Early guide, trail blazer, agent at times for both French and Spanish; Assisted in the founding of East Texas missions
Buried: Natchitoches, LA.

Stamps, Virgil Oliver
1892-1940

Organizer of the Stamps Quartet, Singer; Established largest printing business devoted exclusively to gospel music; President of Texas State Singers Association
Buried: Laurel Land, Dallas.

Standifer, Jacob L.
1818-1902

Veteran of the Battle of San Jacinto, 1st Regiment, Texas Volunteers, Company C
Buried: Elgin, Texas.

Standifer, William Bailey
1812-1876

Veteran of the Battle of San Jacinto; 1st Regiment, Texas Volunteers, Company C (Jesse Billingsley's company)
Buried: Hog Eye Cemetery, 3 miles SW of Elgin.

Stapp, Elijah
1783-1843

Signer of the Texas Declaration of Independence, from Virginia
Buried: Russell Ward Cemetery, 5 miles NW of Edna.

Stark, Henry Jacob
1887-1965

Heir to one of country's greatest lumber fortunes; Engaged in farming, banking, real estate, oil drilling; Philanthropist to education and culture
Buried: Orange, Texas.

Starr, James Harper (M.D.)
1809-1890

"Financier of the Republic of Texas." Surgeon General of the Republic (1839), On the 1st board of regents of U. T.
Buried: Greenwood Cemetery, Marshall.

Starr, Richard
-1836

Perished defending the Alamo, March 6, 1836, of 25
Buried: with the heroes of the Alamo.

Steele, Alphonso
1817-1911

Veteran of the Battle of San Jacinto, 2nd Regiment, Texas Volunteers, 6th Company
Buried: Mexia.

Stephens, Ashley
-1836

Killed at the Battle of San Jacinto
Buried: on the field at San Jacinto.

Stephens, William
-1836

Massacred as one of Fannin's men at Goliad
Buried: Goliad.

Sterrett, William Greene
1849-1924

Journalist for the **Dallas Morning News**, 1st Texas journalist to be assigned the Washington, D. C. office
Buried: Greenwood Cemetery, Dallas.

Sterling, Ross Shaw
1875-1949

Governor of Texas (1931-1933), Highway program with slogan, "Bring Texas out of the mud"; Oilman, Philanthropist to T.C.U. and Boys Home
Buried: Glenwood Cemetery, Houston.

Stevens, Abraham
-1836

Massacred as one of Fannin's men at Goliad
Buried: Goliad.

Stevenson, Coke Robert
1888-1975

Governor of Texas (1941-1947), Soil conservation, Veterans' land program; His 87 vote loss to LBJ for Senate seat closest race in nation's history

	Buried: on his ranch at Telegraph near Junction in Kimble County.
Stevenson, James P.	Organized the first Protestant Church in Texas Buried: McMahan's Chapel 5 miles south of Geneva.
Stevenson, William *1768-1857*	Early Methodist preacher near Nacogdoches, 1st Protestant minister to preach in Texas Buried: Claiborne Parish, LA.
Stewart, Charles Bellinger (M.D.) *1806-1885*	Signer of the Texas Declaration of Independence, from South Carolina Buried: Montgomery, Texas.
Stewart, Charles B. *-1836*	Massacred as one of Fannin's men at Goliad Buried: Goliad.
Stewart, James E. *-1836*	Perished defending the Alamo, March 6, 1836, at age of 28 Buried: with the heroes of the Alamo.
Stewart, John C. *-1836*	Killed at the Battle of Refugio in the Texas Revolution Buried: Mt. Calvary Cemetery, Refugio.
Stillman, Charles *1809-1837*	Operator of steamboats on the Rio Grande River; Founder of the city of Brownsville Buried: City Cemetery, Brownsville.
Stillwell, William S. *1809-1837*	Veteran of the Battle of San Jacinto, Artillery Buried: Founders' Memorial Park, Houston.
Stockton, Richard L. *-1836*	Perished defending the Alamo, March 6, 1836, at age of 18.
Stollenwerck, Logan Henry *1902-1971*	Educator, public school teacher and administrator; S. M. U. football great (1921-24), Quarterback of the "Aerial Circus" (1st SWC team to utilize the forward pass), All SWC for 3 years,

Captain of championship team
Buried: Sparkman-Hillcrest, Dallas.

Stovall, Joseph A.
-1836
Massacred as one of Fannin's men at Goliad
Buried: Goliad.

Strake, George William
1894-1969
Pioneer oilman, Opened the Conroe field; Philanthropist
Buried: Garden of Gethsemane Cemetery, Houston.

Strunk, Bennett
-1836
Massacred as one of Fannin's men at Goliad
Buried: Goliad.

Stubenrauch, Joseph W.
1852-1938
Botanist who developed many varieties of peaches adaptable to the Texas climate
Buried: Mexia.

Summerlin, A. Spain
-1836
Perished defending the Alamo, March 6, 1836, at age of 19
Buried: with the heroes of the Alamo.

Summers, William E.
-1836
Perished defending the Alamo; One of 32 from Gonzales who went to help defend the Alamo, at age of 24
Buried: with the heroes of the Alamo.

Sumners, Hatton William
1875-1962
Congressman from Texas for 34 years, Fought FDR's "Packing the Supreme Court"
Buried: Garland.

Sutherland, John (M.D.)
1792-1867
Sent by Travis to rally people of Gonzales to support the Alamo; Wrote an account of the Alamo Battle
Buried: Sutherland Springs.

Sutherland, George
1787-1855
Veteran of the Battle of San Jacinto; 1st Regiment, Texas Volunteers, Company D
Buried: Texana, Jackson County.

Sutherland, William D.
-1836
Perished defending the Alamo, March 6, 1836, at age of 18
Buried: with the heroes of the Alamo.

Swearengen, Elemeleck
1805-1887

Veteran of the Battle of San Jacinto; Company B, Regular Infantry
Buried: homestead 8 miles from Sealy, Texas.

Swearingen, William C.
-1839

Veteran of the Battle of San Jacinto; 1st Regiment, Texas Volunteers, Company B, Regular Infantry
Buried: Founders' Memorial Park, Houston.

Sweeny, Thomas Jefferson
1812-1869

Veteran of the Battle of San Jacinto, 2nd Regiment, Texas Volunteers, 4th Company, Infantry
Buried: Sweeny family cemetery, Sweeny, Brazoria County.

Swisher, James Gibson
1794-1864

Signer of the Texas Declaration of Independence, from Tennessee, Veteran of the Siege of Bexar
Buried: Oakwood Cemetery, Austin.

Swisher, John Melton
1819-1891

Veteran of the Battle of San Jacinto; 1st Regiment, Texas Volunteers, Company H; Texas Ranger
Buried: Oakwood Cemetery, Austin.

Sylvester, James Austin
1807-1882

Color Bearer at the Battle of San Jacinto, Capturer of Santa Anna
Buried: originally in Odd Fellows Cemetery, New Orleans; Moved through the efforts of Lou Kemp to the State Cemetery, Austin.

Taliaferro, Benjamin W.
-1836

Massacred as one of Fannin's men at Goliad
Buried: Goliad.

Tarrant, Edward H.
1799-1858

Early colonist, Texas Ranger, General, Helped to drive Indians from present day Fort Worth area; Tarrant County named for him
Buried: Pioneer Rest Cemetery, Fort Worth.

Tatom, Joseph R.
-1836

Massacred as one of Fannin's men at Goliad
Buried: Goliad.

Tatom, Memory B.
-1836

Massacred as one of Fannin's men at Goliad
Buried: Goliad.

Taylor, Campbell
1812-1888

Veteran of the Battle of San Jacinto, 1st Regiment, Texas Volunteers, Company C
Buried: Bastrop.

Taylor, Charles Stanfield
1808-1865

Signer of the Texas Declaration of Independence, from England
Buried: Oak Grove Cemetery, Nacogdoches.

Taylor, Edward
-1836

Perished defending the Alamo, March 6, 1836, at age of 18
Buried: with the heroes of the Alamo.

Taylor, George
-1836

Perished defending the Alamo, March 6, 1836, at age of 22
Buried: with the heroes of the Alamo.

Taylor, James
-1836

Perished defending the Alamo, March 6, 1836, at age of 20
Buried: with the heroes of the Alamo.

Taylor, Kneeland
-1836

Massacred as one of Fannin's men at Goliad
Buried: Goliad.

Taylor, William S.
-1869

Veteran of the Battle of San Jacinto, 2nd Regiment, Texas Volunteers, Company J, Cavalry
Buried: City Cemetery, Montgomery.

Teich, Frank
1856-1939

"Father of the granite industry in Texas," Brought Pompeno Coppini to Texas to work on many state monuments and memorials
Buried: Llano.

Temple,
Thomas Lewis Latane
1859-1935

Lumberman and Industrialist, Developed the Southern Pine Lumber Company, Philanthropist
Buried: Texarkana.

Terry, Benjamin Franklin
1821-1861

Member of Austin's Old 300; Leader of Terry's Texas Ranger, Killed in the

service of the Confederate Army
Buried: Glenwood Cemetery, Austin.

Thayer, George J. W.
-1836

Massacred as one of Fannin's men at Goliad
Buried: Goliad.

Thomas, B. Archer M.
-1836

Perished defending the Alamo, March 6, 1836, at age of 19
Buried: with the heroes of the Alamo.

Thomas, David
1801-1836

Signer of the Texas Declaration of Independence, from Tennessee
Buried: DeZavala Cemetery across Buffalo Bayou.

Thomas, Evans B.
-1836

Massacred as one of Fannin's men at Goliad
Buried: Goliad.

Thomas, Henry
-1836

Perished defending the Alamo, March 6, 1836, at age of 25
Buried: with the heroes of the Alamo.

Thompson, Algernon P.
1818-1873

Veteran of the Battle of San Jacinto, William Fisher's Company; Writer and publisher
Buried: Houston (grave is lost).

Thompson, Ben
1842-1884

Outlaw, Killed in San Antonio with "King" Fisher
Buried: Oakwood Cemetery, Austin.

Thompson, Henry Livngston
-1837

Commodore of the Texas Navy
Buried: Founders' Memorial Park, Houston.

Thompson, Jesse G.
-1836

Perished defending the Alamo, March 6, 1836
Buried: with the heroes of the Alamo.

Thompson, J. N.
-1843

Victim of the Mier Expedition
Buried: Monument Hill, LaGrange.

Thomson, John W.
-1836

Perished defending the Alamo, March 6, 1836, at age of 25
Buried: with the heroes of the Alamo.

Thorn, Frost
1793-1854

Minor empresario
Buried: Nacogdoches.

Thorn, John Stephen
-1836

Massacred as one of Fannin's men at Goliad
Buried: Goliad.

**Thornton,
Robert Lee ("Bob")**
1880-1964

Dallas banker and civic leader, Philanthropist
Buried: Restland, Dallas.

Thrall, Homer S.
1819-1894

Methodist minister, Prolific writer on theology and Texas, Wrote 1st school history for the State in 1876
Buried: San Antonio.

**Throckmorton,
James Webb (M.D.)**
1825-1867

Governor of Texas (1866-1867), Removed by U. S. Military as an impediment to Reconstruction
Buried: Pecan Grove Cemetery, McKinney.

Thurston, John M.
-1836

Perished defending the Alamo, March 6, 1836, at age of 27, Rank of second lieutenant
Buried: with the heroes of the Alamo.

Ticknor, Issac
-1836

Massacred as one of Fannin's men at Goliad
Buried: Goliad.

Tierwester, Henry
1795-1859

Veteran of the Battle of San Jacinto, 1st Regiment, Texas Volunteers, Company I
Buried: Houston.

Tilson, Lewis
-1836

Massacred as one of Fannin's men at Goliad
Buried: Goliad.

Tindall, William M.
-1893

Veteran of the Battle of San Jacinto; Regular Infantry, Company A
Buried: Eastland.

Tinkle, Julien Lon
1906-1980

Professor of Comparative Literature, SMU, Former President of The Texas Institute of Letters, Managing Editor of the Southwest

Review, Book Critic for **The Dallas Morning News**, Author of many works, including: **Thirteen Days To Glory; The Valiant Few, J. Frank Dobie** and **Mr. De**
Buried: Hillcrest Memorial Park, Dallas.

Tippit, J. D.
1924-1963

Veteran Dallas policeman allegedly shot and killed by Lee Harvey Oswald on the same day that Kennedy was assassinated
Buried: Laurel Land, Dallas.

Tips, Kern
1904-1967

Well known sportscaster, Announced football games for 32 years; "The Voice of the Southwest Conference," especially U. T.
Buried: Houston.

Tobin, Edgar
1896-1954

Flier in World War I, Member of Eddie Rickenbacker's "Hat in the Ring" squad; Killed in the same plane crash that took the life of Thomas Elmer Braniff Buried: Sunset Memorial Park, San Antonio.

Toepperwein, Adolph
1869-1962

Texas Sports Hall of Fame for Marksmanship
Buried: Mission Burial Park, San Antonio.

Toler, Robert A.
-1836

Killed at the Battle of Refugio in the Texas Revolution
Buried: Mt. Calvary Cemetery, Refugio.

Tom, John Files
1818-1906

Veteran of the Battle of Concepcion, the Grass Fight, the Siege of Bexar; Seriously wounded at the Battle of San Jacinto
Buried: Leakey, Edwards County.

Torrey, James N.
-1843

Victim of the Mier Expedition
Buried: Monument Hill, LaGrange.

Torrey, John F.
1821-1893

Pioneer promoter of Texas industry
Buried: New Braunfels.

Townsend, Everett Ewing
1871-1948

Texas Ranger, "Father of the Big Bend National Park"
Buried: Alpine.

Trammel, Burke
-1836

Perished defending the Alamo, March 6, 1836, at age of 26
Buried: with the heroes of the Alamo.

Trask, Olwyn J.
-1836

Killed at the Battle of San Jacinto
Buried: on the field at San Jacinto.

Travis, William Barrett
1809-1836

Lawyer, Leader of the War Party, Lt. Colonel commanding the Texas forces at the Alamo, Perished there at the age of 27
Buried: with the heroes of the Alamo.

Trigg, Edna Westbrook
1868-1946

Texas' first home demonstration agent, Encouraged pressure cooking, Organized girls' tomato clubs
Buried: IOOF Cemetery, Denton.

Trimble, Edward
-1842

Killed at the Dawson Massacre
Buried: Monument Hill, LaGrange.

Trost, Henry Charles
1860-1933

Outstanding Texas architect
Buried: El Paso.

Troutman, Johanna
1817-1880

"The Betsy Ross of Texas", Created the 1st Revolutionary flag (general); Flag used 1st at Velasco, Destroyed at Goliad
Buried: State Cemetery, Austin.

Truett, George Washington
1867-1944

Most outstanding Baptist minister and leader of his day, Pastor of 1st Church in Dallas for nearly 50 years
Buried: Hillcrest, Dallas.

Tumlinson, George Washington
-1836

Perished defending the Alamo; One of 32 who went from Gonzales to help defend the Alamo, at age of 27
Buried: with the heroes of the Alamo.

Turbeville, Wilkins S.
-1836

Massacred as one of Fannin's men at Goliad
Buried: Goliad.

Turnbull, James *-1843*	Victim of the Mier Expedition Buried: Monument Hill, LaGrange.
Turner, Amasa *1800-1877*	Veteran of the Battle of San Jacinto; Regular Infantry, Company B Buried: Masonic Cemetery, Gonzales.
Tyler, John *-1836*	Massacred as one of Fannin's men at Goliad Buried: Goliad.
Tyson, Paul *1886-1950*	Texas Sports Hall of Fame for Football, In 21 years of coaching: 167 W, 30 L, 9 T Buried: Waco.
Usher, Patrick *1801-1843*	Veteran of San Jacinto and the Mier Expedition Died of starvation in Perote Prison, Mexico, on August 23, 1843.
Vandiver, Harry Schultz *1882-1973*	Internationally known mathematician; Professor at U. T. Buried: Memorial Park, Austin.
Van Zandt, Isaac *1813-1847*	Lawyer, Republic of Texas leader, Instrumental in Texas joining the Union; VanZandt County named for him Buried: Marshall.
Varner, Martin	Member of Austin's Old 300; Owner of the first distillery in Texas Buried: Hickory Point near Independence.
Vaughan, James *-1836*	Massacred as one of Fannin's men at Goliad Buried: Goliad.
Vaughan, William E. *-1836*	Massacred as one of Fannin's men at Goliad Buried: Goliad.
Vigal, George Marion *-1836*	Massacred as one of Fannin's men at Goliad Buried: Goliad.

Vinson, Robert Ernest
1876-1945

Minister, Professor of Theology at U. T. in Austin, President of U. T. (1916-1923); Fought Governor Ferguson over appropriations for the University
Buried: Sherman.

Viven, John
-1856

Veteran of the Battle of San Jacinto; 1st Regiment, Texas Volunteers, Company A (William Ward's)
Buried: Founders' Memorial Park, Houston.

Volckman, Frederick J.
-1836

Massacred as one of Fannin's men at Goliad
Buried: Goliad.

Wade, Houston
1882-1947

Researcher and writer on Texana; One of the founders of the Sons of the Republic of Texas; Advocate of historical markers
Buried: Fayetteville, Texas.

Wade, John M.
1815-1879

Veteran of the Battle of San Jacinto, Artillery
Buried: Travis County.

Wadsworth, William A. O.
-1836

Massacred as one of Fannin's men at Goliad
Buried: Goliad.

Waevenskjold, Elise Amaline Tvede
1815-1895

Norwegian social worker and reformer, Leader in the 4 Mile Prairie community in VanZandt County, Lived there for 46 years
Buried: Lutheran Cemetery 4 Mile Prairie near Prairieville, TX.

Waggoner, William
-1836

Massacred as one of Fannin's men at Goliad
Buried: Goliad.

Waggoner, William Thomas
1852-1934

Early cattleman, banker, philanthropist; Built Arlington Downs
Buried: Fort Worth.

Walker, Asa
-1836

Perished defending the Alamo, March 6, 1836, at age of 23
Buried: with the heroes of the Alamo.

Walker, Jacob
-1836

Perished defending the Alamo, March 6, 1836, at age of 31; probably the last person to die there
Buried: with the heroes of the Alamo.

Wallace, A. J.
-1836

Massacred as one of Fannin's men at Goliad
Buried: Goliad.

Wallace, Benjamin C.
-1836

Massacred as one of Fannin's men at Goliad
Buried: Goliad.

Wallace, Samuel P.
-1836

Massacred as one of Fannin's men at Goliad
Buried: Goliad.

Wallace, William Alexander Anderson ("Big Foot")
1817-1899

Veteran of the Somervell and the Mier Expedition imprisoned in the Castle of Perote; Texas Ranger; 6'2" 240 lbs.
Buried: State Cemetery, Austin.

Waller, Edwin
1800-1883

Signer of the Texas Declaration of Independence, from Virginia; Veteran of the Battle of Velasco; 1st mayor of Austin
Buried: State Cemetery, Austin.

Walling, Henry
-1843

Victim of the Mier Expedition, Was wounded 15 times by the firing squad before finally killed by pistol shot
Buried: Monument Hill LaGrange.

Walling, Jesse
1794-1866

Veteran of the Battle of San Jacinto, 2nd Regiment, Texas Volunteers, 1st Company, Infantry
Buried: Walling Bend Cemetery, 6 miles from Whitney, Texas.

Walsh, Charles Clinton
1867-1943

Writer, Civil servant, On the commission that established S.M.U., "Poet Laureate of the Southwest"
Buried: San Angelo.

Walthall, Wallace Wales
1881-1970

Pioneer in the motion picture business (1915); His brother, Henry, played in D. W. Griffith's **Birth of a Nation**
Buried: Restland, Dallas.

Ward, John
-1836

Killed at the Battle of Refugio in the Texas Revolution
Buried: Mt. Calvary Cemetery, Refugio.

Ward, Thomas William
1807-1872

Veteran of the Siege of Bexar (lost his right leg there) and the Battle of San Jacinto; Lost his right arm while firing a cannon to celebrate Texas independence (1841); Participant in the Archives War, Fired on by Eberley; Land commissioner for the Republic of Texas
Buried: Austin.

Ward, William
-1836

Dispatched by Fannin to relieve Amon B. King at Refugio; Captured by Urrea, taken to Goliad and executed with the rest of Fannin's men
Buried: Goliad.

Ward, William B.
-1836

Perished defending the Alamo, March 6, 1836, at age of 30, Rank of sergeant
Buried: with the heroes of the Alamo.

Ware, William
1800-1853

Veteran of the Battle of San Jacinto, 2nd Regiment, 2nd Company, Rank of Captain
Buried: Waresville Cemetery, 1 mile N of Uvalde.

Warnell, Henry
-1836

Perished defending the Alamo, March 6, 1836, at age of 24
Buried: with the heroes of the Alamo.

Washington, Joseph G.
-1836

Perished defending the Alamo, March 6, 1836, at age of 28
Buried: with the heroes of the Alamo.

Washington, Lawrence A. (M.D.)
1814-1882

Grandnephew of George Washington
Buried: Fairview Cemetery, Denison.

Waters, Nicholas B.
-1836

Massacred as one of Fannin's men at Goliad
Buried: Goliad.

Water, Thomas
-1836

Perished defending the Alamo, March 6, 1836, at age of 24
Buried: with the heroes of the Alamo.

Watson, Joseph W.
-1836

Massacred as one of Fannin's men at Goliad
Buried: Goliad.

Waugh, Beverly
1789-1858

1st Methodist Bishop of Texas
Buried: Mt. Olivet Cemetery, Baltimore.

Weaver, Alman
-1836

Massacred as one of Fannin's men at Goliad
Buried: Goliad.

Webb, James
-1836

Massacred as one of Fannin's men at Goliad
Buried: Goliad.

Webb, Walter Prescott
1888-1963

Outstanding Texas historian, 45 years on the faculty at U. T., Director of the Texas State Historical Association, Wrote or edited over 20 books
Buried: State Cemetery, Ausitn.

Weedon, George
-1842

Veteran of the Battle of San Jacinto; 1st Regiment, Texas Volunteers, Company I
Buried: State Cemetery, Austin.

Weiser, Harry Boyer
1887-1950

Among the world's best known colloidal chemists, Professor of chemistry at Rice, Chemical warfare in World War I
Buried: Houston.

Welch, Robert Alonso
1827-1952

Oilman, Banker, Businessman in sulphur industry and real estate, Philanthropist
Buried: Glenwood Cemetery, Houston.

Wells, Francis F. (M.D.)
1800-after 1850

Member of Austin's Old 300
Buried: Texana, Jackson County.

Wells, James
1817-1840

Veteran of the Battle of San Jacinto, 2nd Regiment, Texas Volunteers, Cavalry
Buried: Old City Cemetery, Houston.

Wells, Norman Miles
-1842

Killed at the Dawson Massacre
Buried: Monument Hill, LaGrange.

Wells, William
-1836

Perished defending the Alamo, March 6, 1836, at age of 22
Buried: with the heroes of the Alamo.

Wentzner, Christian G.
-1852

Veteran of the Battle of San Jacinto; 1st Regiment, Texas Volunteers, Company F
Buried: near Ellenger 6 miles SE of LaGrange.

West, Claiborne
1800-1866

Signer of the Texas Declaration of Independence, from Tennessee
Buried: Riverside Cemetery, Seguin.

West, James
-1836

Massacred as one of Fannin's men at Goliad
Buried: Goliad.

Weston, Thomas
-1836

Massacred as one of Fannin's men at Goliad
Buried: Goliad.

Westover, Ira
-1836

Massacred as one of Fannin's men at Goliad
Buried: Goliad.

Whaling, Henry
-1843

Drew a black bean (Mier Expedition) and was executed
Buried: Monument Hill, LaGrange.

Wharton, John Austin
1809-1838

Adjutant general, On Houston's staff at the Battle of San Jacinto, "Wielded the best blade at San Jacinto"; Congressman of the Republic
Buried: State Cemetery, Austin.

Wharton, William Harris
1806-1839

Veteran of the Siege of Bexar, President of the 1833 Convention, Commission to U. S. for aid with Austin and Archer

Buried: Wharton family cemetery, Clute, Brazoria County.

Wheeler, Orlando
-1836

Massacred as one of Fannin's men at Goliad
Buried: Goliad.

Wheeler, Samuel L.
-1880

Veteran of the Battle of San Jacinto; 1st Regiment, Texas Volunteers, Company B
Buried: Fort Bend County.

White, Edward H. II
1930-1967

Outstanding young American, Logged over 4,236 hours flight time, U. S. Astronaut, Pilot for Gemini 4, 1st astronaut to be outside space craft with hand held maneuvering, One of only 3 men to die while on duty with the U. S. Space Program, Senior pilot for Apollo I when killed in space craft fire at Cape Kennedy
Buried: Arlington National Cemetery.

White, Isaac
-1836

Perished defending the Alamo, March 6, 1836
Buried: with the heroes of the Alamo.

White, Robert
-1836

Perished defending the Alamo; One of 32 from Gonzales who went to help defend the Alamo, at age of 30, rank of lieutenant
Buried: with the heroes of the Alamo.

White, Walter

Member of Austin's Old 300
Buried: Richmond, Brazoria County.

Whitesides, James
1771-1848

Member of Austin's Old 300
Buried: Independence.

Whittaker, Madison G.
1811-1893

Veteran of the Battle of San Jacinto, 2nd Regiment, Texas Volunteers, 1st Company, Infantry
Buried: Old North Church, Nacogdoches.

Wilder, James S.
-1836

Massacred as one of Fannin's men at Goliad
Buried: Goliad.

Wigfall, Louis Trezevent
1816-1874

Civil servant, Leader for Southern rights, Aide to General Beauregard, Opposed Jefferson Davis' military plans, Favored General Lee
Buried: Episcopal Cemetery, Galveston.

Wills, James Robert (Bob)
1905-1975

Outstanding folk singer and recording star, Leader of Bob Wills and the Texas Playboys, The song **San Antone Rose** one of their biggest hits
Buried: Memorial Park in Tulsa, OK.

Wilkenson, Freeman
-1839

Veteran of the Battle of San Jacinto; 2nd Regiment, Texas Volunteers, 5th Company (Thomas McIntire's)
Buried: San Jacinto State Park, Houston.

Wilkenson, James G.
1805-1848

Veteran of the Battle of San Jacinto; 1st Regiment, Texas Volunteers, Company H
Buried: State Cemetery, Austin.

Wilkey, Henry
-1836

Massacred as one of Fannin's men at Goliad
Buried: Goliad.

Williams, Abner B.
-1836

Massacred as one of Fannin's men at Goliad
Buried: Goliad.

Williams, Amelia Worthington
-1958

Brilliant researcher and writer, Professor of history, Recognized for critical study of Alamo Battle
Buried: Little River Cemetery, Maysfield, Milam County.

Williams, James
-1836

Massacred as one of Fannin's men at Goliad
Buried: Goliad.

Williams, Leonard Houston
1800-1856

Indian agent for Houston, Negotiator with Indians not to fight during Texas Revolution, Ransomed many whites for Indians; Lost an eye in the battle at San Antonio
Buried: Old Dr. Pitts Cemetery, Mount Calm, Limestone County.

Williams, Napoleon B.
-1836

Massacred as one of Fannin's men at Goliad
Buried: Goliad.

Williams, Samuel May
1795-1858

Close friend and private secretary of Stephen F. Austin; Founder of Texas Masonry; Member of Austin's Old 300
Buried: Galveston.

Williams, William F.
1816-1878

Veteran of the Battle of San Jacinto, 2nd Regiment, Texas Volunteers, 1st Company, Infantry
Buried: Kosse-Bremond Cemetery 2-1/2 miles from Kosse, Falls County.

Williamson, Hiram J.
-1836

Perished defending the Alamo, March 6, 1836, at age of 26, rank of sergeant-major Buried: with the heroes of the Alamo.

Williamson, Robert McAplin ("Three-legged Willie")
1806-1859

Veteran of the Battle of San Jacinto 2nd Regiment, Texas Volunteers, Company J, Cavalry
Buried: State Cemetery, Austin.

Wilmans, Edith Eunice Therrel
1882-1966

1st woman elected to the Texas Legislature (1922), Democratic Party leader
Buried: Sparkman-Hillcrest, Dallas.

Wilmouth, Louis
1806-1893

Veteran of the Battle of San Jacinto; 2nd Regiment, Texas Volunteers, 8th Company, Infantry
Buried: Harshberg Cemetery near Sadler, Grayson County.

Wilson, David L.
-1836

Perished defending the Alamo, March 6, 1836, at age of 29
Buried: with the heroes of the Alamo.

Wilson, James
-1844

Veteran of the Battle of San Jacinto, 2nd Regiment, Texas Volunteers, 2nd Company
Buried: Founders' Memorial Park, Houston.

Wilson, John
-1836

Perished defending the Alamo, March 6, 1836, at age of 32
Buried: with the heroes of the Alamo.

Wilson, Robert W.
-1836

Massacred as one of Fannin's men at Goliad
Buried: Goliad.

Wilson, Samuel
-1836

Massacred as one of Fannin's men at Goliad
Buried: Goliad.

Winburn, McHenry
-1847

Veteran of the Battle of San Jacinto, 1st Regiment, Texas Volunteers, Company D
Buried: Round Top, Texas.

Wing, Martin Carroll
-1843

Victim of the Mier Expedition
Buried: Monument Hill, LaGrange.

Wingate, Edward
-1836

Massacred as one of Fannin's men at Goliad
Buried: Goliad.

Winn, James C.
-1836

Massacred as one of Fannin's men at Goliad
Buried: Goliad.

Winningham, William S.
-1836

Massacred as one of Fannin's men at Goliad
Buried: Goliad.

Winship, Stephen
-1836

Massacred as one of Fannin's men at Goliad
Buried: Goliad.

Winter, Andrew
-1836

Massacred as one of Fannin's men at Goliad
Buried: Goliad.

Winters, Christopher
-1836

Killed at the Battle of Refugio in the Texas Revolution
Buried: Mt. Calvary Cemetery, Refugio.

Winters, James Washington
1817-1912

Last surviving veteran of the Battle of San Jacinto; 2nd Regiment, Texas Volunteers, 2nd Company

Buried: Brummett Cemetery, 3 miles E of Big Foot, Frio County.

Winters, John Frelan
1814-1864

Veteran of the Battle of San Jacinto; 2nd Regiment, Texas Volunteers, 2nd Company
Buried: 2 miles NE of Hawthorne, Walker County.

Winters, William C.
1834-1860

Veteran of the Battle of San Jacinto; 2nd Regiment, Texas Volunteers, 2nd Company
Buried: Hopkinsville, Gonzales County.

Winters, William
1809-1863

Wounded at the Battle of San Jacinto; 2nd Regiment, Texas Volunteers, 2nd Company
Buried: Brummett Cemetery 3 miles E of Big Foot, Frio County.

Wirty, Alvin Jacob
1888-1951

Lawyer, Texas Senator, Developer of river power to generate electricity, Oil and Water law; Early backer of LBJ, On canvass committee declaring LBJ winner over Stevenson
Buried: State Cemetery, Austin.

Withers, Harry Clay
1880-1959

"Dean of the Texas newspaper editors," **Dallas Morning News** and other papers
Buried: Sparkman-Hillcrest, Dallas.

Witt, Hughes
-1836

Massacred as one of Fannin's men at Goliad
Buried: Goliad.

Wolcott, Fred
1916-1972

Texas Sports Hall of Fame for Track, Won 7 national AAU championships, Won 5 NCAA championships, World's greatest hurdler, Attended Rice
Buried: Forest Park Westheimer, Houston.

Wolfe, Anthony
-1836

Perished defending the Alamo, March 6, 1836
Buried: with the heroes of the Alamo.

Wood, George T. *1795-1858*	Second governor of Texas (1847-1849), Senator, Veteran of the Mexican War Buried: Point Blank, 15 miles E of Huntsville.
Wood, Henry H. *-1836*	Massacred as one of Fannin's men at Goliad Buried: Goliad.
Wood, John *-1836*	Massacred as one of Fannin's men at Goliad Buried: Goliad.
Wood Samuel *-1836*	Massacred as one of Fannin's men at Goliad Buried: Goliad.
Wood, Samuel *-1836*	Killed at the Battle of Refugio in the Texas Revolution Buried: Mt. Calvary Cemetery, Refugio.
Wood, William *-1854*	Veteran of the Battle of San Jacinto; 1st Regiment, Company A Buried: Houston.
Wood, William P. *-1836*	Massacred as one of Fannin's men at Goliad Buried: Goliad.
Woods, James B. *1802-1851*	Signer of the Texas Declaration of Independence, from Kentucky Buried: Waelder Ranch Cemetery, 3 miles E of Liberty.
Woods, Zadock *-1842*	Killed at the Dawson Massacre Buried: Monument Hill, LaGrange.
Wren, Allen *-1836*	Massacred as one of Fannin's men at Goliad Buried: Goliad.
Wright, Claiboren *-1836*	Perished defending the Alamo; One of 32 from Gonzales who went to help defend the Alamo, at age of 26 Buried: with the heroes of the Alamo.

Wright, Isaac Newton
-1836

Massacred as one of Fannin's men at Goliad
Buried: Goliad.

Wright, Gladys Yoakum

Born in Greenville, Wrote the words to the state song, **Texas Our Texas**
Buried: St. Louis, MO.

Wright, Rufus
-1876

Veteran of the Battle of San Jacinto, 1st Regiment, Texas Volunteers, Company I
Buried: Live Oak County.

Wyly, Alfred Henderson
-1867

Veteran of the Battle of San Jacinto, 2nd Regiment, Texas Volunteers, Infantry (company unknown)
Buried: Hempstead, Waller County.

Wynne, Angus Gilchrist
1886-1975

Attorney, Oilman, Business leader, Philanthropist
Buried: Grove Hill, Dallas.

Y Barbo, Antonio Gil
1729-1809

Founder of the city of Nacogdoches
Buried: Old Spanish Cemetery, Nacogdoches.

Yeamans, Elias Robert
-1836

Massacred as one of Fannin's men at Goliad
Buried: Goliad.

Yoakum, Henderson King
1810-1856

Writer, Authority on Texana, Friend of Sam Houston
Buried: Huntsville.

Young, Harrison
-1836

Massacred as one of Fannin's men at Goliad
Buried: Goliad.

Young, James O.
-1836

Massacred as one of Fannin's men at Goliad
Buried: Goliad.

Young, William Foster
1800-1876

Veteran of the Battle of San Jacinto, 2nd Regiment, Texas Volunteers, Company J. Cavalry
Buried: Midway, Madison County.

Youngblood, Solomon
-1836

Massacred as one of Fannin's men at Goliad
Buried: Goliad.

Zaharias, Mildred Ella ("Babe") (Nee Didrickson)
1914-1956

Texas Sports Hall of Fame, Greatest woman athlete of first half of 20th Century, Olympic gold medals for field and track, and basketball
Buried: Beaumont.

Zanco, Charles
-1836

Perished defending the Alamo, March 6, 1836, at age of 28, rank of lieutenant
Buried: with the heroes of the Alamo.

Zavala, Adina Emilia de
1861-1955

Grandaughter of Lorenzo de Zavala; Public school teacher; She, with others, organized one of first societies composed of women for patriotic purposes in Texas (society later affiliated with Daughters of the Republic of Texas); One of her greatest contributions was the purchase of the Alamo property from a wholesale grocery firm, thus saving the Shrine. Member of the Texas Historical Board; An original member of the Committee of One Hundred appointed to plan for a state centennial. Instrumental in the preservation and marking of many historical sites
Buried: St. Mary's Cemetery, Austin.

Zavala, Lorenzo de Jr.

Aide-de-camp to Houston at the Battle of San Jacinto
Buried: Merida, Yucatan Peninsula, Mexico.

Zavala, Manuel Lorenzo de
1789-1836

Leader in both the Mexican and the Texas Revolutions, Ad Interim Vice President of the Republic of Texas
Buried: Buffalo Bayou across from San Jacinto Battleground.

Zuber, William Physich
1820-1913

Texas soldier and historian
Buried: Iola, Texas.

Zumwalt, Andrew
1817-1886

Veteran of the Battle of San Jacinto
Buried: Denton Creek Cemetery 6 miles NE of Gonzales.

TEXANS BURIED ELSEWHERE

In the list of important Texans whose places of rest are known, many are located outside the boundaries of the former Republic. Yet, they had their moment of contribution and deserve to be among those listed. Therefore, the following are those who did contribute to Texas history and, although they rest elsewhere, their memory abides with us always in Texas.

Anderson, Monroe Dunaway
1873-1939

Owner with his brother, Frank, and Will L. Clayton of Anderson Clayton and Co., the leading cotton merchandising firm in the world; Established the M. D. Anderson Foundation in 1936, Led to the funding of M. D. Anderson Hospital in Houston (Texas Medical Center)
Buried: Riverside Cemetery, Jackson, TN.

Andrews, Stephen Pearl
1812-1886

Lawyer, Abolitionist, Writer
Buried: New York.

Atz, Jake
1879-1945

Texas Sports Hall of Fame of Baseball, Manager
Buried: New Orleans, La.

Badgett, Jessi B.
1807-

Signer of the Texas Declaration of Independence, From North Carolina
Buried: Body returned to Arkansas.

Bastrop, Baron Felipe Enrigue Neri de
1766-1827

Native of Holland, Prussian soldier under Frederick the Great; Saw service under the King of Spain, Established colonies in the New World, Greatly aided Moses Austin with Spanish government; Later great benefactor to Stephen F. Austin in his colonization efforts, Land commissioner for SFA
Buried: Saltillo, Mexico.

Bean, Peter Ellis
(or Ellis P)
1783?-1846

Member of Philip Nolan's expedition to Texas, Captured soon after and imprisoned in Mexico until joined the revolutionary Morelos. Formed a group to invade Texas, Fought at Battle of New Orleans; In 1823 settled on Mound Prairie in East Texas, Opposed Hayden Edwards in Fredonian Affair, Indian agent
Buried: Jalapa, Mexico.

Belo, Alfred Horatio
1839-1901

Executive of the **Dallas Morning News**
Buried: Salem, NC.

Bonney, William
1859-1881

Billy, the Kid
Buried: Military Cemetery, Ft. Sumner, NM.

Borden, Gail, Jr.
1801-1874

One of the surveyors of Stephen Austin's Colony, Helped lay out town of Houston; Founder of newspaper, **Telegraph and Texas Register**, 1st collector of customs in Texas, Inventor of condensed milk, Trustee of society which founded Baylor University
Buried: Woodlawn Cemetery, New York, NY.

Bowie, Rezin P.
1793-1841

Joined brothers John J. and James, in slave smuggling
Buried: New Orleans, LA.

Cabell, Charles Pearre
1903-1971

Graduate of West Point, Career Air Force, Rank of General, Veteran of WWII
Buried: Arlington National Cemetery.

Carson, Samuel Price
1798-1838

Signer of the Texas Declaration of Independence, From North Carolina
Buried: Hot Springs, AR (unmarked grave).

Chennault, Claire Lee
1890-1958

Born in Commerce Texas; Related paternally to Sam Houston and maternally to Robert E. Lee; Career Army, Rank of General; Flying veteran of WWII, Organizer and head of the

"Flying Tigers"
Buried: Arlington National Cemetery.

Chisholm, Jessee
-1868

Trail driver, guide, plainsman
Buried: Blaine County, OK.

Dabney, Robert Lewis
1820-1898

Presbyterian minister, Confederate Army chaplain with Stonewall Jackson until illness forced him out of service; Co-founder of the Austin School of Theology; Was blind the last 8 years of his life
Buried: Cemetery of Union Theological Seminary, Hampden-Sidney, Virginia.

Everitt,
Stephen Hendrickson
1807-1844

Signer of the Texas Declaration of Independence, from New York
Buried: New Orleans.

Fisher, John
1800-1865

Signer of the Texas Declaration of Independence, from Virginia; Brother of William S. Fisher, the commander of the Mier Expedition
Buried: Hollywood Cemetery, Richmond, VA.

Fitzhugh, John P. T. (M.D.)
1815-1877

Veteran of the Battle of San Jacinto, Assistant Surgeon, 1st Regiment, Texas Volunteers
Buried: Warren County, Mississippi.

Flourney, George M.
1832-1889

Attorney General when Houston was deposed, Confederate sympathizer
Buried: California.

Gaines, James
1776-1856

Signer of the Texas Declaration of Independence, from Virginia
Buried: Quartsburg, California.

Gregg, John
1828-1864

Confederate Army general from Texas; 7th Regiment, Texas Volunteers; Killed in service of CSA
Buried: Aberdeen, MS.

Gustine, Lemuel
1816-1852

Veteran of the Battle of San Jacinto; 2nd Regiment, Texas Volunteers
Buried: New Orleans.

Hamilton, Robert
1783-1843

Signer of the Texas Declaration of Independence; Native of Scotland; Financially experienced, personally wealthy, his extensive connections helped Texas during the Revolution
Buried: Saratoga Springs, NY.

Handy, W. C.
1873-1958

Composer and Pianist; His songs include **The St. Louis Blues, Memphis Blues** and **Beale Street Blues**
Buried: Woodlawn Cemetery, Bronx, NY.

Hawkins, Charles E.
-1837

First Commander of the Texas Navy
Buried: New Orleans.

Hays, John Coffee ("Jack")
1817-1883

Texas Ranger, Indian fighter, Veteran the Mexican War, Surveyor who laid out the city of Oakland, California
Buried: Piedmont, CA.

Hewetson, James
1797-1870

Empresario
Buried: Saltillo, Mexico.

Hirsch, Maximillian Justice
1880-1969

Texas Sports Hall of Fame, World famous jockey and horse trainer
Buried: Floral Park, Long Island, New York.

Hoblitzelle, Karl St. John
1879-1967

Dallas businessman, Civic leader, Philanthropist
Buried: Bel Fontaine Cemetery, St. Louis, MO.

Holley, Mary Austin
1784-1846

Writer, editor and friend of Texas; Cousin of Stephen F. Austin
Buried: St. Louis Cemetery, New Orleans.

Hood, John Bell
1831-1879

Confederate Army general from Texas, Leader of Hood's Texas Brigade, Lost his right leg in battle
Buried: New Orleans.

Houston, Temple Lea
1860-1905

Brilliant trial lawyer, Eccentric in dress, Son of Sam and Margaret Lea Houston; Died in Topeka, Kansas
Buried: Woodward, OK.

Huddle, William Henry
1847-1892

Well-known painter of historical scenes such as **Surrender of Santa Anna** and of portraits such as **David Crockett** and executive of Texas
Died in Austria.

Hurd, William A.
-1838

Successful captain in the Texas Navy, Captured Cuerro Bravo .
Buried: New Orleans, LA.

Huston, Felix
1800-1857

General in the Texas Army, Indian Dueled with Albert Sidney Johnston in 1837
Buried: Washington, MS.

Joplin, Janis Lyn
1943-1970

The "Judy Garland of Rock — Hippie Queen of Show Busienss," Born in Port Arthur
Died and Cremated in Hollywood.

Joplin, Scott
1868-1917

Undisputed king of ragtime music, 1st song was **Maple Leaf Rag**, Composer of the music used in the movie **The Sting**, Born in Texarkana
Buried: St. Michael's Cemetery, New York, NY.

Ketchum, Thomas Edward ("Blackjack")
1863-1901

Outlaw born at Knickerbocker, Texas; Was decapitated when hanged
Buried: Clayton, NM.

Knickerbocker, Hubert Renfro
1898-1949

Internationally known writer and journalist, Pulitzer Prize winner
Killed in plane crash near Bombay, India.

Lacey, William Demetris
1808-1848

Signer of the Texas Declaration of Independence from Virginia
Buried: Paducah, KY.

Langenheim, William
1816-1874

Veteran of the Siege of Bexar, Captured with of F. W. Johnson at San Patricio and imprisoned; Photographer
Buried: Philadelphia, PA.

Lindsley, Henry Dickinson
-1938

First national commander of the American Legion, World War I Army colonel, Decorated; Texas Attorney,

Banker, Mayor of Dallas (1913)
Buried: Arlington National Cemetery.

Lubbock, Thomas S.
1817-1862

Veteran of the Siege of Bexar and the Somervell Expedition, Succeeded Terry as leader of Terry's Texas Rangers, Died in the service of the Confederate Army
Buried: Kentucky.

Lucas, Anthony Francis
1855-1921

Geologist, Authority on the structure of salt domes, Oil explorer, 1st Lucas gusher: 1901 opening the Spindletop Oil Field
Died in Washinton, D. C.

Mangrum, Lloyd
1914-1973

Texas Sports Hall of Fame for Golf
Buried: Apple Valley, CA.

McClelland, Samuel
-1843

Veteran of the Battle of San Jacinto, the Mier and Somervell Expeditions
Buried: Hacienda St. John, Laguna Saco, Mexico.

McCloskey, John J.
1862-1940

Texas Sports Hall of Fame for Baseball, Administration
Buried: Louisville, KY.

Molyneaux, Peter
1882-1953

Journalist, lecturer and writer who championed free trade and Southern conservatism; Published **The Texas Weekly**
Buried: New Orleans.

Moore, Edwin Ward
1810-1865

2nd Commander of the Texas Navy
Died in New York City.

Moore, Francis, Jr. (M.D.)
1808-1864

Geologist, Geographer, Lawyer, Promoter of H & TC Railroad, Purchaser of **Telegraph and Texas Register**
Buried: Brooklyn, NY.

Muldoon, Father Miguel

Priest in Austin's Colony (1823-1842) Burial place unknown somewhere in Mexico, Commemorative marker in Hostyn, Texas.

Munger, Robert Sylvester
1854-1923

Pioneer in improvement of ginning machinery in the U. S., Real estate developer in Dallas, Munger Place is named for him
Buried: Birmingham, AL.

Murphree, David
1811-1866

Veteran of San Jacinto, Member of Houston's staff, Veteran of Somervell Expedition
Buried: Missouri.

Murphy, Audie Leon
1924-1971

Most decorated soldier of World War II, Movie star, Grew up in Farmersville-Celeste area of east Texas
Buried: Arlington National Cemetery.

Murrah, Pendleton
-1865

Governor of Texas (1863-1865) during the Civil War, Administration ended with the fall of the Confederacy
Buried: Panteon Municipal Cemetery N1, Monterey, Mexico.

Myers, Elijah E.
1832-1909

Architect of present Capitol Building in Austin
Buried: Detroit, Michigan.

Nimitz, Chester, William
1885-1966

Fleet Admiral of the U. S. Navy during World War II, On board the USS Missouri during the Japanaese surrender
Buried: Golden Gate National Cemetery, San Bruno, CA.

Padilla, Fray Jaun de
-1544

Franciscan missionary, Accompanied the Coronado Expedition, Returned to serve Indians in the Panhandle; 1st Christian martyr of Texas when he ventured past Quivira and was killed by Indians
Buried: Unknown in Kansas.

Parker, Cynthia Ann
1827-1864

Captured by the Comanche Indians when 9 years old, Raised by Indians and married Peta Nocona, Mother of his 2 sons (Pecos and Quanah) and 1 daughter (Prairie Flower); Recaptured by white man in 1860
Buried: Cache, OK.

Perry, James H. (D.D.)
1811-1862

Veteran of San Jacinto, Volunteer-aide, Methodist minister. After the Revolution re-entered the ministry in New York
Buried: Brooklyn, NY.

Porter, William Sydney (O. Henry)
1862-1910

Writer and author; Convicted of embezzling bank funds where he was a teller, he was sent to prison (1898-1902); Adopted pseudonym while in prison
Buried: New York City.

Post, Charles William
1854-1914

Creator of Post Toasties and Postum; Purchased large land blocks in West Texas and founded the city of Post ; He colonized some 1200 people there
Buried: Santa Barbara, CA.

Post, Wiley
1899-1935

Internationally known aviator and explorer; Lost sight in right eye when hit by a piece of metal while drilling an oil well; Piloted the **Winnie Mae** around the world in 8 days, 15 hours, and 51 minutes (1931); Crashed at Point Barrow, Alaska, with Will Rogers on board; Both were killed
Buried: Memorial Park Cemetery, Edmond, OK.

Rankin, Melinda
1811-1888

Early, avid Protestant missionary in Texas
Buried: Bloomington, IL.

Rickard, George L. (Tex)
1871-1929

Texas Sports Hall of Fame for Boxing
Buried: New York City.

Robinson, James W.
1800-

Veteran of San Jacinto, Cavalry Company
Buried: San Diego, CA.

Rosenberg, Henry
1824-1893

Banker, Philanthropist, Founder of an orphans' home, Civic leader in Galveston, City of Rosenberg named for him
Buried: Loudon Park Cemetery, Baltimore, MD.

Ruby, Jack
(Jake Rubenstein)
1911-1967

Assassinator of Lee Harvey Oswald (November 24, 1963)
Buried: Westlawn Cemetery, Chicago.

Seguin, Juan Nepomuceno

Veteran of the Battle of San Jacinto
Buried: Santiago, Mexico.

Sheridan, Ann
(Clara Lou Sheridan)
1915-1967

Famous movie and television star, From Denton
Buried: Hollywood, CA.

Short, Walter Campbell
1880-1949

Major general, U. S. Army, at Pearl Harbor, December 7, 1941, "Scapegoat" of sneak attack
Buried: Arlington National Cemetery.

Smith, Henry
1788-1851

Veteran of the Battle of San Jacinto; Early leader of the War Party; Provisional governor (1835-1836); Defeated in try for office of President of Texas (1836); Died in a mining camp in Los Angeles County, California

Smithwick, Noah
1808-1899

Veteran of the Battle of Concepcion; Texas Ranger; Published **The Evolution of a State**
Died in Santa Ana, California

Snively, Jacob
1809-1871

Rank of colonel, Leader of the Snively Expedition, Prospector and Miner; Killed by Indians
Buried: Gillette, AZ.

St. Denis,
Louis Juchereau de
1676-1744

Early guide, trail blazer, agent at times for both French and Spanish; Assisted in the founding of East Texas missions
Buried: Natchitoches, LA.

Stevenson, William
1768-1857

Early Methodist preacher near Nacogdoches, 1st Protestant minister to preach in Texas
Buried: Claiborne Parish, LA.

Waugh, Beverly
1789-1858

1st Methodist Bishop of Texas
Buried: Mt. Olivet Cemetery, Baltimore.

White, Edward H. II
1930-1967

Outstanding young American, Logged over 4,236 hours flight time, U. S. Astronaut, Pilot for Gemini 4, 1st astronaut to be outside space craft with hand held maneuvering, One of only 3 men to die while on duty with the U.S. Space Program, Senior pilot for Apollo I when killed in space craft fire at Cape Kennedy
Buried: Arlington National Cemetery.

Wills, James Robert (Bob)
1905-1975

Outstanding folk singer and recording star, Leader of Bob Wills and the Texas Playboys, The song **San Antonio Rose** one of their biggest hits
Buried: Memorial Park in Tulsa, OK.

Wright, Gladys Yoakum

Born in Greenville, Wrote the words to the state song, **Texas Our Texas**
Buried: St. Louis, MO.

Zavala, Lorenzo de Jr.

Aide-de-camp to Houston at the Battle of San Jacinto
Buried: Merida, Yucatan Peninsula, Mexico.

SOURCES NOT PREVIOUSLY CITED

Basic References:

Adair, A. Garland. **Texas Pictorial Handbook**. Austin: Texas Heritage Foundation, 1957.

Allen, Tom. **The Sage of Texas**. Garland: Van-Wood Publishing Co., 1964. Also the bibliography at the conclusion of the work.

The author's personal notes and files.

Bugbee, Lester G. "The Old Three-Hundred: A List of Settlers in Austin's First Colony." **Quarterly of the State Historical Association**, Volume No. 1, issue No. 2. Austin: Texas Historical Association, October 1897, 108-117.

County and Cemetery Records of Angelina, Austin, Bexar, Brazoria, Brazos, Bureleson, Chambers, Cherokee, Collin, Colorado, Dallas, Denton, Fayette, Fort Bend, Galveston, Grimes, Harris, Jackson, Jefferson, Kaufman, LaVaca, Matagorda, Nacogdoches, Tarrant, Travis, Van Zandt, Waller, Washington and Wharton Counties.

Dixon, Sam Houston, and Louis Wiltz Kemp. **The Heroes of San Jacinto**. Houston: The Anson Jones Press, 1932.

Neff, Pat Morris, and Louis Wiltz Kemp. **Monuments**. Austin: Board of Historians of the Centennial, 1936.

Webb, Walter P., et al., eds. **The Handbook of Texas**. Austin: The Texas Historical Association, 1952.

Williams, Amelia. "A Critical Study of the Siege of the Alamo." **Southwestern Historical Quarterly:**
Volume No. 36, issue No. 4, chapter 1, 251-287, April, 1933.
Volume No. 37, issue No. 1, chapter 2, 1-44, July, 1933.
Volume No. 37, issue No. 2, chapter 3, 79-115, October, 1933.
Volume No. 37, issue No. 3, chapter 4, 157-184, January, 1934.
Volume No. 37, issue No. 4, chapter 5, 237-312, April, 1934.

Secondary Sources

Castenada, Carlos E. **Our Catholic Heritage in Texas**. Austin: Von Bolckmann-Jones Co., 1936-1958.

Duval, John C. **Early Times in Texas**. Austin: H. P. N. Gammel and Co., 1892.

Smithwick, Noah. **Evolution of a State, or Recollections of Old Time Texas**. Austin: The Steck Publishing Co., 1935.

Texas Almanac, Editors of **The Dallas Morning News** and **The Galveston News** from 1857 through 1979.

Files of **The Dallas Morning News, The Galveston News** and **The Houston Telegraph**.

Files of the **Texas Historical Quarterly** and the **Southwestern Historical Quarterly**.